An Introduction to Firearms

An Introduction to Firearms

Your Guide to Selection, Use, Safety, and Self-Defense

James Morgan Ayres

Skyhorse Publishing

Skyhorse Publishing books may be purchased in bulk at special discounts for sales promotion, corporate gifts, fund-raising, or educational purposes. Special editions can also be created to specifications. For details, contact the Special Sales Department, Skyhorse Publishing, 307 West 36th Street, 11th Floor, New York, NY 10018 or info@skyhorsepublishing.com.

Skyhorse® and Skyhorse Publishing® are registered trademarks of Skyhorse Publishing, Inc.®, a Delaware corporation.

Visit our website at www.skyhorsepublishing.com.

10 9 8 7 6 5 4 3 2 1

Library of Congress Cataloging-in-Publication Data is available on file.

Cover design by Owen Corrigan
Cover photo by Lindsey K. Breuer
Interior photos, except chapter 2 and where noted, © ML Ayres.
Chapter 2 photos, except where noted, © Justin Ayres.

Print ISBN: 978-1-62873-679-3
Ebook ISBN: 978-1-62914-111-4

Printed in China

Table of Contents

Foreword by Mykel Hawke

I have watched the TTPs, or Tactics, Techniques, and Procedures, change a lot over thirty years. The principles always remain the same. The styles come and go in and out of fashion and often come back full circle. What I like about Mr. Ayres's book, *An Introduction to Firearms*, is that its core principles are universal and eternal. There is great information in here for the beginner right up to the expert. For a great read for any level, sure to be insightful and informative as well as an entertaining read, this is a must have for any firearms user.

—Mykel Hawke, author of *Hawke's Green Beret Survival Manual*, star of Discovery Channel's *Man, Woman, Wild* and Travel Channel's *Lost Survivors*, and Special Forces Captain (retired) and combat commander

Introduction

Welcome to the fraternity of shooters. We are a widely diverse group that includes men, women, and children; doctors and lawyers; car mechanics, homebuilders, and bakers of bread; and millions of folks from all walks of life. The fraternity sprawls worldwide and is open to all of good intent. People from countries all over the world collect firearms, shoot competitively, and hunt, and you'll find something in common with many of them.

Some of us are gun nerds—like computer nerds—who are so far into the intricacies of the gun we cannot understand anyone who doesn't share our enthusiasm. Some are professional soldiers or law enforcement officers, military or former military, but the great majority are regular folks who enjoy the shooting sports or collect guns, much like others collect art, stamps, or French wine.

This book goes a fair distance beyond the basics and introduces the first-time gun owner, or the gun owner with limited experience, to many uses of the gun, such as hunting, sporting competition, and self-defense. Given the critical nature of self-defense, this book contains considerable detail on effective self-defense with firearms.

I have been a gun user for a half-century, have never yet had an accidental discharge, and generally hit what I aim at. I've never shot anything I didn't mean to shoot. I've successfully hunted small and large game on four continents, and I have been obliged to defend myself and others in armed conflicts in various countries. From this experience, I've arrived at some conclusions about guns and their usage. My intent in giving you a bit of my history is not to impress you with my background and knowledge, which is meager and undistinguished when compared to some others, but rather to let you know that the information in this book comes from someone qualified to write on the subject. There are experts on various aspects of the gun and its usage whose opinions differ from mine. I cannot say they are wrong, because their experience has led them to their own conclusions. But based on my own experience I can, and on occasion do, respectfully disagree with them.

Stories are often remembered long after dry facts have faded away. I have included a few stories to illustrate certain points, as well as to entertain and stimulate reflection; all of them are taken from life. My editor suggested that for this book I write in an informal voice, like an uncle talking to a nephew or niece who is interested in getting into some aspect of guns and shooting, and I have endeavored to do so. I hope you find the information in this book to be helpful if you decide to take to the field in pursuit of game, or to the range in pursuit of that perfect score, and that you never have to use any of these skills in defense of your life or those of your loved ones.

Firearms Terminology

ACP:

An acronym for Automatic Colt Pistol, it refers to cartridges designed to be fired in automatic pistols, such as .45 ACP, .380 ACP, .25 ACP, etc.

Action:

The part of the firearm that places rounds into the chamber.

Artillery Piece:

A combat arm used by armed forces to discharge large projectiles of various kinds, including explosive and illuminating rounds, also known as cannon or big guns.

Automatic:

Generally refers to both fully-automatic firearms and semiautomatic firearms. Fully-automatic firearms will continue to fire as long as the trigger is held back until the magazine is empty. Semiautomatic firearms fire one shot each time the trigger is pulled.

Barrel:

The tube of a gun through which projectiles pass and by which they are directed to their target.

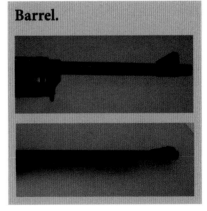

Barrel.

Beaters:

The people who are sent ahead of the shooters to beat the bushes and drive out animals so they can be shot in certain kinds of hunting. For example, English wing-shooting and tiger hunting in India.

Bolt:

A sliding rod that chambers and ejects rounds in a bolt-action firearm.

Bolt-Action:

A firearm that uses a manually operated bolt to chamber a round, also known as a bolt gun.

Bore:

The inside of the barrel of a gun.

Box Magazine:

A magazine that resembles a box and can be removed from a firearm.

Bullet:

The projectile portion at the top of the cartridge.

Butt:

The bottom of the stock of a shoulder firearm, the part that touches the shoulder.

Buttplate:

A plate covering the butt; in military firearms it is usually steel, in civilian firearms usually rubber.

Caliber:

A measurement, either in inches or millimeters, of the inside of a rifled barrel.

Carbine:

A lightweight shoulder firearm similar to a rifle but significantly shorter.

Centerfire:

Type of ammunition that has a primer in the center of the base of the cartridge.

Chamber:

A tightly fitted area just behind the barrel where the bullet is placed (chambered) in preparation for being struck by the firing pin.

Chambering:

1. To put a round in the chamber. 2. Another term for caliber. For example, "chambered for a forty-five," or "forty-five is a good chambering."

Cocked:

When the hammer or firing pin is ready to drop.

Bullet.

Butt. © Winchester

Buttplate of a shoulder weapon. ©Winchester

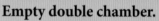

Empty double chamber.

Shells chambered in a double chamber.

Double Barrel:
A rifle or shotgun with two barrels, which can be arranged side-by-side or with one over the other. Usually referred to as side-by-side or over-under.

Double Action:
A mechanism in which the hammer or firing pin is cocked by the movement of the trigger.

A hammer ready to drop.

Failure to Feed:
See "Malfunction."

Firing Pin:
A pin or protrusion of steel that strikes the primer of the cartridge, thereby igniting (firing) the cartridge. A firing pin may be contained in a bolt or situated on a hammer.

FMJ:
A full metal jacket is any bullet made of a lead core covered with brass, steel, or other metal.

Forearm:
A support under the barrel where the hand is placed that is commonly made of wood or synthetic material.

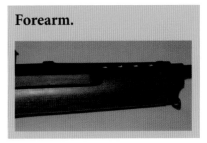
Forearm.

Garand:
The M1 Garand is the standard battle rifle of the US Army in World War II and Korea; it is named for its designer, John Garand.

Gauge:
A measurement of the inside diameter of a shotgun barrel.

Grip:
The handle of a handgun.

Grip.

Group:
A number of bullet holes in close proximity to each other, commonly measured by the distance between the two holes that are farthest apart. For example, two-inch group or three-inch group.

Gun:

Everybody has seen the movie where the marine drill instructor makes a recruit run around like an idiot screaming, "This is my rifle, this is my gun . . . ." Properly speaking, a gun is a smoothbore—which lacks rifling—or an artillery piece. But common usage labels all firearms guns. So we'll call them guns, too. Just don't join the Marines and tell your drill instructor I told you it was okay to call a rifle a gun; it won't help you to avoid the consequences.

Gun Nerds:

Gun nerds are so far into the objects of their devotion that, like computer nerds, they often have no real-world application for the device and are simply fascinated by the working of it. (Not to be confused with gunnies.)

Gunny:

A non-gender-specific term referring to gun enthusiasts; also a term of respect, as the Marine gunnery sergeants are the highest ranking enlisted men and the best Marines. (Not to be confused with gun nerds.)

Hammer:

The device that strikes the primer of a cartridge thereby firing it.

Handgun:

Firearms designed to be fired with one hand that have no attached shoulder stock. Handguns are also commonly referred to as pistols; however, properly speaking a pistol is a semiautomatic, not a revolver. (Handguns are also commonly fired using two hands, but they are not referred to as handsguns.)

Handguns: Beretta Model 20 .25 and FN Five-seveN semiautomatic.

Hardball:

An old gunnie's term for .45 ACP FMJ.

Hollowpoint:

A bullet with a cavity at the point, designed to expand.

Hoppe's No. 9:

A cleaning solvent that removes cartridge residue from the bore and other parts of a gun. It has been in use for many years, some say since the Napoleonic Wars or possibly longer. It has a distinctive scent that gun nerds and even some gunnies consider comparable to Chanel No. 5.

Iron Sights:

Standard metal sights, not optical.

JHP:
Jacketed hollow point, a hollow-point bullet, usually lead, with a brass, steel, or other metal jacket or covering.

Lands and Grooves:
Commonly referred to as "rifling," the spiral cuts inside a barrel that affect the bullet as it passes through the barrel.

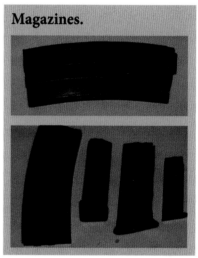
Lever-action rifles.

Lever-Action:
A type of action in which the cartridges are chambered by manipulating a lever.

Magazine:
1. A device that holds cartridges in the firearm before they are chambered. Magazines may be detachable or integral. 2. A term for a building in which munitions are stored.

Magazines.

Malfunction:
A failure of a cartridge to feed into the chamber, eject from it, or otherwise operate properly.

Magazine Release:
A button or lever that releases a detachable magazine from the firearm.

Manual of Arms:
The correct procedures for handling any given weapon.

Magazine release.

Misfire:
An event that occurs when the firing pin or hammer strikes the primer but fails to ignite it.

Muzzle:
The front of the barrel where the projectile emerges.

Muzzle.

Performance Envelope:
The expected limits of performance of any kind of system or mechanism. For example, the performance envelope of a service handgun could include specifications such as the ability to deliver accurate fire at twenty-five yards and the ability to operate with one hand.

Push–Pull Method:

A two-handed method of gripping a handgun whereby one hand pushes against the force exerted by the other hand, the idea being to stabilize the handgun and control recoil.

Race Guns:

High performance custom guns designed for competition.

Receiver:

The part of the gun that houses the chamber and related parts.

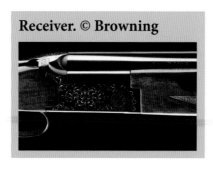

Receiver. © Browning

Another example of a receiver.

Recoil:

The backward or upward reaction or movement of a firearm when it is fired.

Red Dot Scope:

An optical sight on a firearm that superimposes a red dot on the target.

Revolver:

Handguns with a cylinder containing a number of chambers. Each chamber houses a round and is revolved into firing position by the pull of the trigger, in the case of a double-action revolver, or by manually cocking, usually with the thumb, the hammer of a single-action revolver. Double-action revolvers can also be revolved and cocked manually.

Double-action revolver.

Rifle:

A firearm designed to be fired from the shoulder with lands and grooves, commonly referred to as "rifling," cut into the interior of the barrel. This rifling imparts spin to the projectile, stabilizing it and enabling accuracy.

Rifle.

Rimfire:

Ammunition that contains the primer in the rim of the cartridge.

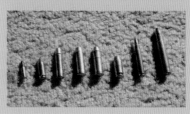

Rounds/cartridges.

Round:

One cartridge or one shot. Derived from the term used to describe one round of fire from the days of muskets and single-shot rifles.

Safe Action:

A term coined by Glock (an Austrian firearms manufacturer), to describe their proprietary trigger, which is a hybrid but functions as a double-action.

Safety ON.   Safety OFF.

Safety:

A device designed to block the trigger or firing pin to prevent accidental discharge of the gun. There are various types of safeties, many of which are specific to a particular firearm.

Scope:

An accessory mounted on a firearm to optically increase the apparent size of anything viewed through the sight.

Semiautomatic:

A firearm that uses the energy of a fired round to chamber the next round. A true automatic can fire many rounds with one press of the trigger. A semiautomatic requires the trigger to be pressed each time a round is to be fired. A very few pistols have selector switches which allow the shooter to fire in full automatic mode. Almost everyone calls a semiautomatic handgun an automatic, so we will also.

Semiautomatics: Walther PPK and FN Five-seveN

Service Handgun:

Handguns suitable for use by military or law enforcement, usually large caliber automatics.

Shotgun:

A firearm distinguished by having no lands or grooves. Shotguns are smoothbores and are designed to shoot, primarily, a number of round pellets commonly know as "shot," therefore: shotgun. The pellets are contained in one cartridge and discharged with one pull of the trigger. Shotguns can also fire slugs, solid projectiles similar to rifle bullets but much larger. Lacking rifling, no spin is imparted to the slug and they are less accurate than rifle bullets.

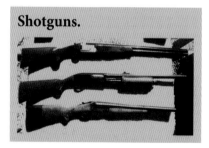

Shotguns.

Sights.

Aperture/peep sight.
©Tech-SIGHTS, LLC

Sight(s):

Devices that enable accurate aiming of a gun.

Sight, Aperture, or Peep:

A hole through which the shooter looks to center the front sight and focus on the target.

Sight, Front:
Commonly, a post or bead that the shooter aligns with the rear sight to focus on the target.

Front sight.

Sight(s), Open:
Various kinds of open notches the shooter aligns with the front sight to focus on the target.

An example of open sights.

Sight, Telescopic:
An accessory mounted on a firearm to optically increase the apparent size of anything viewed through the sight.

Slide:
The part of an automatic that moves back and forth to chamber another round when the gun is fired.

Smoothbore:
Another term for a shotgun due to its lack of rifling.

Solid:
A solid bullet, as opposed to a hollowpoint.

Stock:
The part of a shoulder weapon that is placed to the shoulder or the part of the gun to which the barrel is attached.

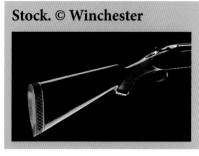
Stock. © Winchester

Stock Weld:
The contact point between the shooter's cheek and the stock.

Striker:
The portion of the firing pin or hammer that strikes the primer.

Cheek weld.

Target:
An object at which the shooter aims that he or she desires the bullet or shot to strike.

Target of Opportunity:
A target discovered serendipitously. A bull's-eye at a shooting range is a formal target. A pinecone on the ground could be a target of opportunity.

Trajectory:
The arc all projectiles describe when fired. Gravity pulls projectiles to earth.

Trigger:

A curved lever that, when pulled, releases the hammer or bolt containing the firing pin.

Trigger Guard:

A loop, often made of metal, attached to the receiver that surrounds the trigger and is designed to protect the trigger from being accidentally tripped.

Windage:

1. The amount of deflection the wind will produce in a projectile. 2. The amount needed to adjust the aim of a projectile to counter wind deflection. 3. The adjustment of sights from side to side.

Wingshooting:

The practice or attempt of shooting birds in flight.

A handgun trigger.

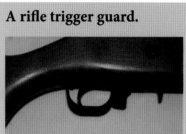
A rifle trigger guard.

Part I:
Gun Selection

CHAPTER 1

A Case for the .22

Your first gun should be a target-grade rifle or handgun chambered for the .22 long rifle (.22LR) cartridge. This used to be gospel. All new shooters were advised to start with this little rimfire. Then something changed—I'm not sure what. This now appears to be a minority opinion, one which some experts today disagree with. I have read that some think it's best to go right to the gun and caliber the new shooter intends to use for big game or self-defense, especially if the object is self-defense.

I believe a foundation of marksmanship laid down with a .22 will better serve a shooter than any other introduction to shooting. About the only exception I can think of would be the shooter who plans to shoot only trap or skeet and never intends to do any other kind of shooting. Even then, starting with a .22 is not a bad thing.

A strong and solid foundation for marksmanship is best built on a few thousand rounds of .22 ammunition expended in fun and in serious practice. There's a good deal more to shooting than hunting and self-defense, but if either of these endeavors is your goal, you won't go wrong starting with a .22. Target shooting—from plinking to Olympic-level benchrest, trap, and skeet—are only a few of the shooting sports that have occupied and entertained millions. Virtually all these activities can be built on a foundation laid down with the lowly .22 rimfire.

Furthermore, the .22 is more than a training round. It is a useful and versatile cartridge. I know more than one person who relies on a .22 for subsistence hunting and others who, for various reasons, have used it for self-defense. (You can find more detailed information about the .22 as it specifically relates to hunting and self-defense in those specific chapters.)

FUN TO SHOOT

Twenty-twos are just plain fun to shoot. They have none of the muzzle blast and recoil that intimidate so many new shooters. I have seen more than one first-time shooter try his or her hand with a large caliber rifle or pistol only to be driven away from the sport forever with ringing ears and a sore shoulder from a Monster Magnum rifle or a stinging palm from that Dirty Harry Colt Detective Special. There's no excuse to not use good ear and eye protection when shooting. However, even with the proper protection, the kick of a full power .44 Magnum revolver can be a bit much for a new shooter, or even some experienced shooters, to deal with.

ACCURACY

Accuracy always matters, but it is especially important when you're learning to shoot. A new shooter should expect to make many mistakes as part of the learning process. He or she will not benefit from a firearm that cannot be relied upon to produce consistent, excellent accuracy. With an inaccurate firearm, a new shooter cannot be sure if a miss is his or her fault or that of the gun. Select one of the .22 handguns or rifles recommended in this chapter, buy good ammo, zero your gun (as explained in the chapter on how to shoot), and you can be sure a miss is yours, not the gun's. With a no excuses gun, you can focus on improving your marksmanship and not worry about the gun.

COST

Twenty-twos have the virtue of being inexpensive to buy and to shoot. A thousand rounds of .22LR ammo costs less than dinner in a cheap restaurant, a car wash in Los Angeles . . . well, you get

the idea. Twenty-twos are cheap to shoot, even if you're buying top quality ammo. The guns are also inexpensive to purchase. Unless you go for a top match-quality or highly decorated pistol or rifle, you can get a .22 that will shoot the ears off a rattlesnake at fifty yards.

EFFECTIVENESS

Make no mistake: the .22 is far more than a training round. It is effective beyond what its limits would appear to be. In part, this is due to good sectional density, which enables it to penetrate well. There are subsistence hunters the world over who use the .22 to take whatever game is available, including large game.

My friend Mike, an Inuit from Alaska, uses a .22 rifle to hunt caribou and moose to feed his family and to kill marauding walruses when they destroy his nets and eat his fish. Caribou and moose are large animals. The technique Mike told me he used was to get very close, ten to fifteen yards, and shoot a burst of at least five rounds into the heart and lungs. He shot walruses, which can weigh four hundred pounds and have sharp foot-long tusks, from about ten feet with headshots. The point is that the .22 is more effective than most people think it is.

The military and various other government agencies also use the .22 to good effect. I was taught to always keep a Bug Out Bag or Ready Bag close at hand in the event that I had to E&E (Evade & Escape) and found myself in a survival situation. I was to always keep in my BOB a match-grade .22 pistol and two hundred rounds of ammunition. The rationale for this specific handgun was that it would take any reasonable game, it was effective as a self-defense weapon, its report was relatively quiet, and the entire package, pistol and ammunition, weighed little. I carried a High Standard Victor in a photographer's shoulder bag along with other useful items. Many .22 pistols are ammunition sensitive; my old High Standard was extremely so. Later on I switched handguns, but not the caliber or the concept.

Today this kind of training is called SERE. Survival, Evasion, Resistance, and Escape training is taught to all elite military units, covert operators, and most pilots. In one military school I am aware of, the trainers and students take everything from frogs to deer with .22 handguns as part of their SERE training. They hunt legally on a military reservation as part of SERE training. In the other instances I write about, the hunters are Native American subsistence hunters who are hunting on Native American land and are within their legal rights.

Make no mistake, the .22 is an effective all-around cartridge. It's good to know that in a survival situation, large game can be taken with a .22. However, do not go out in search of your autumn whitetail with your new .22 handgun or rifle. Doing so would be in violation of virtually all game laws in the United States, and the Fish and Wildlife officers will confiscate your firearm and at the very least fine you. Be sure to check regulations with your local Fish and Game authorities to learn which firearms are legal for the game you pursue. In general, small game is fair game for a .22, but check to make sure.

When you select your .22, be aware that performance will vary with different brands of ammo. You should try as many different variations as you can find to determine which one groups best and is most reliable in your gun. Practice a lot. Without exception, everyone in my Basic Training and Advanced Infantry Training classes who qualified as Expert (which none of us considered a major accomplishment) had owned and shot a .22 since they were kids. There is simply no substitute for expending thousands of rounds for fun without the recoil and muzzle blast of large caliber weapons.

SUGGESTED FIRST GUNS

Start with a .22 and learn it well before graduating to more powerful guns. You'll be glad you did. And, who knows, you may one day be in a situation where that .22 will be just what you need to bring in game.

.22 HANDGUNS – AUTOMATICS

Beretta

This five-century-old company with a well-deserved reputation for making quality firearms makes a space-age-looking .22 called, appropriately, the U22 Neos. I have only used the Neos once; a friend loaned me his, and I sent couple of hundred rounds downrange with no misfires or malfunctions. This is a reasonably accurate handgun and will serve the new shooter well—if the raked grip angle is comfortable for you. Comfort and fit, how the gun *feels* to you, is especially important for a first gun.

Beretta U22 Neos. © Beretta

Browning

Browning's best-known .22 automatic handgun is the Buckmark, which comes in about fifteen variations. All of them that I have used are accurate and reliable and do not seem to be unduly ammunition sensitive. Personally, I like the feel of the Buckmark in my hand. The Buckmark has been in extensive use in SERE training for some years and is well regarded by both instructors and trainees.

Browning Buckmark. © Browning

Ruger

The Mark III Standard is the current generation of a series that had become an American icon. This series has been in production for more than thirty years. It is a solid, well-made, reliable, and accurate handgun that will last for generations if well cared for. It has an enclosed bolt and a grip angle that many find points well for them. Available in

at least a half-dozen versions, all that I have fired shoot well and seem to accept almost any ammo.

Ruger Mark III. © Ruger

The Ruger 22/45 is similar to the Standard except that its grip angle and magazine release matches that of the Model 1911 .45 ACP. In addition, it has a polymer frame and is lighter weight than the Standard. We've had one of these in our family for more than ten years, and during that time it has fired uncounted thousands of rounds through it with no problems. I have found no difference in accuracy or reliability between the Standard and the 22/45. Both the Standard and the 22/45 are in current use at SERE schools and are neck and neck with the Buckmark in popularity.

Ruger 22/45. © Ruger

SIG-Sauer

The Mosquito certainly looks like a Sig. It's lighter weight than others in this category, and given

Sig-Sauer's reputation for excellence, it could be a good choice—if you fire only CCI Mini-Mags in it, as the owner's manual directs. I fired one hundred rounds of the recommended ammo with no problems and with good accuracy. When I tried other types of ammo, the Mosquito repeatedly malfunctioned. Only rely on this handgun if you follow the manufacturer's direction regarding ammo.

SIG-Sauer Mosquito. © Sig Sauer

Smith & Wesson

Currently, Smith & Wesson produces a half-dozen variations of its 22A series. All seem to be well-made, and the few I have shot had accuracy roughly equal to the Ruger pistols and Browning Buckmark. This is one of the handguns in use with some of today's SERE trainers, but it is less tolerant of not being cleaned.

S&W 22A series. © Smith & Wesson

All of these .22 automatics should be able to produce one- to two-inch groups at twenty-five yards from a rest with iron sights—if the shooter does his or her part. They also lend themselves to mounting a scope or red-dot sight, which many shooters choose to do, including the guys at the SERE school mentioned above. There are other pistols that will fill the bill, but these are available at most gun shops and are reasonably priced.

.22 Handguns – Revolvers

Twenty-two revolvers, such as the Smith & Wesson Kit Gun, served generations of outdoorsmen as trail guns. Today Colt, Smith, Ruger, Taurus, and others continue to make high-grade .22 revolvers, including a .22 Magnum—a more powerful rimfire cartridge. The automatics are somewhat easier to master in that they only require you to learn to shoot a single-action trigger. Competent revolver work requires mastery of the double-action trigger. The revolver is slower to fire should you need rapid fire, which you might. The automatic holds more rounds and is much faster to reload. Having the facility to fire ten rounds rapid-fire, reload, and fire another ten rounds in a few seconds is a valuable attribute—one that the revolver lacks. This could be especially important in a firearm of low power.

Automatics are subject to fewer mechanical problems under harsh field conditions. This is one of the reasons the world's military forces use them. If you were to slip while crossing a stream and give your handgun a thorough dunking, drop it in mud, or get sand inside the mechanism, it would be much easier to field strip, dry, and clean an auto than a revolver. Field stripping an auto is, generally speaking, a simple chore. Removing the side plate of a revolver and cleaning out sand, mud, or water from the internal workings is much more complex and time-consuming.

That said, the revolver has its advantages. For those who have difficulty understanding the operation of an automatic, the revolver's mechanism is obvious and can be plainly seen. The revolver is also more tolerant of ammunition than the automatic and will easily shoot high-speed ammo, low-speed ammo, or even shot shells.

.22 RIFLES – SEMIAUTOMATIC

I think the semiautomatic rifle is the best choice for your .22 firearm. The only reason to buy a lever-action .22 is if you have been swept away with the romance of the old West or if it's to be an understudy for a large caliber lever gun. If you're aiming for Olympic competition, start with a good bolt-action .22. You might do the same if your goal is big game hunting, since most big game hunting is done with bolt-action rifles, due to their accuracy and ability to handle powerful ammunition, as well as tradition and the nature of big game hunting in which magazine size is limited by law and the one-shot kill is the goal. If you get into small bore .22 rifle competition, you will need a specialized bolt-action. Otherwise a good, reliable, semiautomatic will serve you best in the field.

Browning

The Browning Semi-Auto 22 (SA22) is a beautiful example of the gunmaker's craft. Introduced in 1987 and popular with those who like the look and feel of well-made traditional firearms, the Browning comes in six levels of finish. Grade I has an attractive walnut stock, traditional bluing, fine checkering, and retails for about $700. Higher grades have more engraving, finer burled walnut stocks, and retail for more than $1500. This rifle is as accurate and reliable as you would expect of any gun bearing the Browning name.

Browning SA22. © Browning

CZ

CZ makes their guns in the Czech Republic with old world craftsmanship and tight tolerances. They are attractive, accurate, and reliable. The 511, which is generally available, shoots as well as the rest of the CZ lineup and is stocked with nice walnut.

Marlin

Marlin enjoys a well-deserved reputation for accuracy, reliability, and quality. They are also a terrific value. Every Model 60 and Model 795 series Marlin I have fired has had outstanding accuracy. This may be due to their well-known Micro-Groove rifling, which is used in all Marlins and the company claims is more precise and accurate than standard rifling. I have used many Marlins over decades of shooting, have never been dissatisfied with any of them, and have found them to be somewhat more accurate than other modestly priced .22 rifles.

Marlin 795. © **Marlin**

The Marlin Model 70PSS Papoose is a takedown rifle that comes with a padded case. The small package can be stored just about anyplace. I have only shot one Papoose, and it, too, possessed the well-known Marlin accuracy.

Remington

The Remington 552 BDL Deluxe Speedmaster is a nicely finished, well-made, accurate rimfire at about twice the price of the Marlin Model 60. It feels heavy and sturdy in the hand, which many feel aids a steady hold.

Remington 552. © **Remington**

The Remington 597 has a plain finish, but retains Remington's manufacturing quality and is priced comparably to the Marlins. This is basically the BDL without the fancy checkering.

Remington 597. © **Remington**

Ruger

Ruger seems to have a knack for designing guns that become classics. The 10/22 Carbine is such a classic, having been in production since 1964. Ruger makes a number of variations on the basic theme, but they're all from the same family and have the Ruger virtues: reliability, durability, and reasonable accuracy.

Savage

The Savage Model 64 is a good rimfire rifle for less than two hundred bucks. From all reports, it's a good shooter. The one I have had experience with shot to point of aim out of the box and looked like it would keep doing so for years.

Of the rifles mentioned above, the Marlins seem to have the best and most consistent accuracy, at least in the models I have shot. Any of these should serve the needs of the new shooter.

Don't think you'll have to put your .22 aside when you learn to shoot. You'll still have many uses for it. There are many true stories of lives being saved with the little rimfire. I can't think of a better tool to store in case of emergencies other than a high-quality .22 and a thousand rounds of ammunition.

CHAPTER 2

Where to Buy Them, Where to Shoot Them

When you buy your first gun, and all the others, do so at a local gun shop. An independent gun shop owner will give you more service, information, and support than you'll ever get online or at the counter of the mass market retailers where the clerk you talk to was selling shoes last week and produce the week before. You might pay a couple of bucks more at, say, Fred & Martha's Shooting Emporium, but you'll get it back, and more with it, in knowledge and help. The people who run independent gun shops, like those who operate bookstores, do so out of love of the thing. None of them are getting rich. You need them in your corner, especially if you're a new shooter.

I took a photo crew with me to a local range with an attached gun shop. The Oak Tree Gun Club, located just north of Los Angeles and open to the public, has ranges for skeet, trap, sporting clays, rifle, and pistol. They offer on-site instruction, and the gun shop has a wide selection of handguns, rifles, and shotguns, as well as a number of antiques. All in all, I thought it would be a good place to shoot—photograph—and show the new shooter what a nice facility was like.

Oak Tree Gun Club Store interior.

There are hundreds of good gun shops all across the country; some of them have similar facilities, some not. I can't visit them all, but Oak Tree is close by and the folks there agreed to let my guys come in and trample over everything with our cameras and questions.

Selection of revolvers at Oak Tree Gun Club Store.

Shawn Eubanks, an employee of the Oak Tree Gun Club Store.

A S&W .500 Magnum for sale.

Walther P38.

A Luger.

While we were there, a small drama played out that couldn't have made my point any better if I had scripted it. All this happened as it is presented. We asked for and received permission from everyone involved to take photos and use their names. You can follow the story in the accompanying photos.

We were bugging the fellow behind the counter with questions and taking pictures of all the cool guns when a young man came in. He said hello to the guy behind the counter, who introduced himself as Shawn Eubanks and shook hands with the customer, Jacobi Wynne.

Jacobi was a clean-cut young fellow with a story of tragedy that is all too common today. He and his family had suffered a home invasion by a criminal gang that resulted in one family member being hospitalized with severe wounds. Jacobi told Shawn he never had any interest in guns and still didn't. He didn't like guns and doubted he would ever shoot one for fun. But he had decided it was incumbent upon him to protect his family and that the only way he could do so was with a firearm.

Shawn Eubanks showing Jacobi Wynn a handgun.

Shawn has worked at Oak Tree since he was fourteen years old. He knows more about guns than the average Marine drill instructor. He could have buried Jacobi in information, but he did not. He patiently discussed Jacobi's needs,

Jacobi Wynn holding a handgun.

abilities, and tolerances. As they talked, Shawn displayed various pistols and revolvers and presented them to his customer to handle. It was immediately apparent that Oak Tree customers were not treated like somebody who dropped in to buy a cabbage on the way home.

Three important points emerged from their conversation. First, Jacobi was not going to become a gun enthusiast at any time in the foreseeable future. Second, he was totally committed to his goal of protecting his family, and he was willing to train as hard as was required to get the expertise he would need. He fully accepted and understood that he needed training and practice to be able to actually use a gun to defend his family. Third, he had no intention of carrying his gun outside his home. Based on Jacobi's commitment and his needs, Shawn guided him to the service pistols.

Shawn told Jacobi that the .45 autos they had been looking at were not for him. "All of us shooters like them, because we can customize them and they're fun to shoot in matches. But they're not right for someone who is not into guns." He then handed Jacobi a Glock. "This is a good gun for people who don't care about guns." He went on to explain the workings of the Glock. He also showed Jacobi the workings of revolvers and explained that they also were good guns for people who don't care about guns. Based on the fact that the home invasion had been carried out by multiple people, Jacobi decided he wanted more rounds available than a revolver provided.

Shawn then showed his customer pistols made by Springfield, Smith & Wesson, and other makers that shared similar characteristics with the Glock: high capacity, simple to operate, and so forth. He emphasized that it was very important that Jacobi should select the one that best fit his hand and that he needed to be comfortable with his choice so he would follow through and do the needed practice.

Shawn spent almost two hours helping his customer decide what gun he needed and counseling him on how to proceed. They narrowed the choices down to two models. Shawn then called the Range Master and asked for an instructor to show Jacobi the basics of shooting a handgun and have him try the pistols at the range before he made his final choice.

Oak Tree firing line.

Within a few minutes, Jacobi was on the firing line with Brian Dillon, a courteous and professional gunny of the first rank and an NRA-Certified Master and Instructor. On the way, the Range Managers, Gene and Doug, helped Jacobi get fixed up with a rental gun and eye and

Entering Oak Tree Gun Club pistol range.

Range Master Brian Dillon illustrating gun handling to Jacobi Wynn.

ear protection. Brian showed Jacobi the ropes: safety, range etiquette, and how to handle, load, and fire a pistol.

Range Master Brian Dillon demonstrating the correct two-hand hold.

Keep in mind that so far, Jacobi had not yet purchased anything other than a bag of ammo and had only spent a couple of bucks to rent a pistol. If he did decide to buy a gun at Oak Tree, the total purchase would be about the price of a week's groceries. I don't know where else you can get that kind of service and professional attention than in a good gun shop.

Shooting instructor Brian Dillon showing the S&W Model 19 to Jacobi Wynn at the firing line.

When Jacobi squeezed off his first round of 9mm, he jumped as if a hand grenade had exploded. It was to be expected: first gun, first shot, loud noise, and recoil. But Brian had shown him how to correctly hold the pistol and control recoil. Jacobi realized that it was just a loud noise, and the bump in his hands didn't really amount to much at all.

He stayed with it. Brian continued to coach him. Jacobi was hitting the target before he expended his first magazine. By the time he had fired ten rounds, he had settled into the work. His determination was palpable. He had no intention of being deflected from his goal by a little noise.

Jacobi Wynn with a S&W automatic.

Jacobi tried two or three different 9mms. He fired about fifty rounds with Brian always at his side talking quietly, encouraging, coaching, and teaching. By the time he had fired his second magazine, he was hitting the

Jacobi Wynn firing a S&W 9mm automatic.

center of his target. Before Jacobi left the Oak Tree facility, he made a decision and bought his first gun. California has a ten-day waiting period. During those ten days, Jacobi can come and practice with his gun on Oak Tree's range. If he wants more professional instruction, it's there for the asking.

Can you even imagine any big box store providing this kind of service for any kind of product? We're talking about a sale that's going to net the company, maybe, forty bucks. As an aside, Brian Dillon is also an archaeologist with a University of California Berkley PhD, a world traveler, witty, friendly, and knowledgeable about a wide range of subjects. Brian made Jacobi feel at home and taught him some important foundational skills.

Everybody at Oak Tree made this new shooter feel comfortable and helped guide him through a difficult and stressful situation. Keep in mind that Jacobi wasn't out for a good time or shopping for a new pair of sneakers. He was making a decision that could affect the future safety of his entire family, and it was clear from

his demeanor that the recent home invasion weighed heavily on him. Where are you going to find people like this to guide you in your first steps as a new shooter if not at your local gun shop or range?

Don't be reluctant to ask for instruction. Even if you have a little experience, you can probably benefit from more training. I had a friend once who had some kind of cognitive disconnect. Roger thought he could outshoot Wyatt Earp, but in fact he couldn't hit a barn with a shotgun if he was inside of it. He wouldn't let me show him anything; he already knew everything there was to know. Eventually, after he shot out the windows in his truck while trying to hit a tin can, he agreed that, maybe, he could benefit from some high-level combat-style shooting lessons from a retired Marine.

My Marine buddy had some time on his hands and agreed to give Roger some basic marksmanship instruction under the guise of jungle combat training, hunter killer sniper training, or something like that. After a little bit of dedicated practice, Roger got good enough so I could take him afield without worrying overmuch about friendly fire.

Most of us can benefit from professional instruction. If you're lucky enough to buy your first firearm from a place that offers instruction, jump at it. If not, contact the NRA and get hooked up with a local instructor. Failing that, almost any good range will have some people hanging around who can show you how to get your rounds on target.

Small bore range. © ML Ayres

Shooter on the firing line with a Walther PPK .380. © ML Ayres

Brian Dillon with an FN Five-seveN. © ML Ayres

Three generations of handguns.

If you're not going to do any of that, then do yourself and the rest of the world a favor. Follow the instructions in this book, and practice until you acquire a reasonable level of competence.

S&W Model 19 & FN Five-seveN.

S&W Model 19.

Almost every region has an informal shooting place within a reasonable distance. Ask the folks at the gun store, club, or shooting range where you can go to do a little informal target practice. At present, I'm based in Los Angeles, one of the largest and most sprawling metroplexes on the planet. Yet, there are dozens of safe shooting areas within an hour's drive.

Los Angeles County recently passed an ordinance that no discharging of firearms was allowed anywhere in the county except at ranges. Sixty minutes and I'm out of the county to where the coyotes howl. I know of legal, safe places to shoot within an hour of Washington DC, Manhattan, and a dozen other cities across the country. The key is to plug into the local shooting fraternity.

An Internet search or a quick look in the yellow pages will turn up gun shops, clubs, and ranges almost anywhere in the country. Don't be shy about dropping in, even if you are not planning to buy anything at the moment. As I said in the introduction, the shooting fraternity is widespread and welcoming to newcomers.

Part II: Gun Use

CHAPTER 3

Foundations of Marksmanship

Marksmanship is the ability to hit what you intend to hit. The fundamentals of marksmanship are simple in description and, at an entry level, relatively easy to attain:

- Identify your target.
- Steady your position.
- Align the sighting system with the target.
- Fire without disturbing the alignment of the sights.

That's about it. Not hard to understand at all; it's hardly magic or rocket science. Actually achieving this goal under any and all field conditions is another matter. Reasonable competence at hitting nonmoving targets at modest ranges can be achieved by anyone in a relatively short period of time—a few hours, maybe a day or two—as long as he or she directs attention to the goal. True mastery takes somewhat longer and can be the practice of a lifetime. The best approach to using this book to learn to shoot is to first read through the entire book, then go back to specific sections and review the detailed instructions.

NATIONAL RIFLE ASSOCIATION BASIC INSTRUCTION

The best possible way to learn is with hands-on instruction. Most areas have local NRA instructors who will show you the basics. You can locate them by going to the NRA website. Some ranges also offer basic instruction or can refer you to an NRA-certified instructor.

ONE GUN

In this section, we'll explore the fundamentals of shooting rifles, shotguns, and handguns, as well as body alignment and grip for a steady hold, trigger control, breathing, sight picture, tracking on moving targets, and more. You'll learn the basics of shooting with sights and without sights. I'll touch on the internal stillness that lasts only a fraction of a second but allows the kind of marksmanship that enables you to shoot quickly, as well as accurately, and can save your life in a lethal encounter.

But here's an important point: start with one gun and learn that gun, whichever one you choose, before trying another gun. It's fine to fire a few rounds from a variety of different guns just to get the feel of them. But once you select your first firearm, stick to it. If you're a beginning shooter, you will find that switching back and forth between firearms *before* you have mastered the first one will make the goal of becoming a marksman more difficult to achieve. At a time when you should be focused entirely on skill development, you will be distracted by variations between the firearms. If you just want to make noise on a Saturday afternoon, then by all means go to your local range and bang away with whatever gun strikes your fancy. But if you're committed to the goal of becoming a good marksman and a safe and responsible shooter, stay with one gun until you have mastered it.

Many people go their whole lives with one or maybe two guns—a rifle and a handgun, perhaps a shotgun. There's a good deal to be said for gaining such a level of familiarity with a particular gun. Operating it becomes as familiar as driving your family car. There's an old saying among shooters, "Beware the one-gun man." All of us who have been around shooting long enough have seen the old guy show up at a local range and shoot the socks off the resident hot

shots with his worn but well-oiled Springfield .30-06 or his old .38 Smith & Wesson revolver with the blue finish worn away.

DRY FIRE

Before shooting live rounds, you should dry fire your gun. First, make sure the gun is unloaded. Put your ammo away. Then, even though you know it's unloaded, do not point your gun at anyone. **Remember: treat all guns as loaded.** Follow the instructions on how to shoot as if you were firing a loaded gun. Do not take your ammo from where you have stored it until you have finished practice. **If you reload your firearm, do not continue to practice.**

One advantage of dry fire is the opportunity to gain familiarity in handling your gun without expending any ammunition. Another is that it provides a means to check your hold and trigger squeeze. For example, it is easy to miss the fact that you are jerking the trigger when you are firing live rounds.

A good practice exercise is to balance a coin on your front sight or barrel and squeeze the trigger as if you were firing a live round. If the coin does not move, you've got a steady hold and a smooth squeeze. It the coin falls when you squeeze the trigger, you do not. Continue to focus and practice until the coin does not fall when you squeeze the trigger. Snap at least a hundred dry rounds with full concentration to get your muscle memory grooved in. You will come back to this practice time and time again. Many good shooters fire ten dry rounds for every live round.

ZEROING YOUR GUN

Before commencing shooting practice, you must ensure that your gun is shooting to point of aim. To do so, you must zero your gun. First, set a target in a safe location with a backstop. A good range is best for this, but you can accomplish the same thing if no range is available. Bull's-eye targets are best for zeroing.

Take a steady rested position. If no shooting bench is available, use one of the positions explained later in this book. Prone is the most steady. If you cannot get steady enough in prone, use an informal rest, such as a tree limb, at least until you can improve your prone position. For the zero to be valid you *must* shoot from a steady position.

Prone position. © Justin Ayres

Get a good sight picture (correct alignment of the sights with the target) on the center of your bull's-eye. Fire three rounds, pausing to get a sight picture for each shot. Take your time. Fire the tightest group you can. Chances are the group will not be centered in the bull. However, if it is centered, fire three more rounds to confirm. If all six rounds are centered in your bull's-eye, the gun you are shooting is zeroed for that load at that distance.

If your three round group is not centered, you must adjust your sights. Following the directions for your particular gun and sight, first adjust your windage left or right to the point where you think your round will be in line with the bull. Fire three rounds and check the group. If you are now directly above or below the bull, you are ready to adjust elevation. If not, repeat until you have a centered group.

Now adjust your sights' elevation up or down—again following the directions for your particular gun and sight—so your group, to the best of your judgment, will be centered. Fire three rounds. If your group is centered, fire another three rounds to confirm. If all six rounds are centered, you are zeroed with this gun and load. If after doing this your group is not centered, rest and repeat the process until your gun is shooting where you aim.

PRACTICING WITH BULL'S-EYE TARGETS

You should practice shooting the bull's-eye at various distances and utilizing all the shooting positions you wish to master. Bull's-eyes don't lie. They are tough taskmasters. Shooting bulls is your basic training. You should invest at least five hundred rounds in this kind of shooting. Practice until you can shoot three tight shot groups from all positions you wish to master at all reasonable distances.

CALLING YOUR SHOTS

By the time you have fired about a hundred rounds, you should be able to call your shot. This means you should know where your shot is going at the moment the hammer, or striker, hits the primer—before your round hits the target. You should be able to look at your target after your shot for confirmation of what you already know.

INFORMAL PRACTICE

Wandering through woods and shooting at pinecones and other targets of opportunity creates a familiarity with your gun and a level of shooting proficiency that little else can equal. As soon as you have attained a level of expertise on bulls-eyes, but not before, start with informal targets and targets of opportunity.

Find a secure location where you can shoot without endangering anyone. This kind of practice is much easier to engage in if you're shooting a .22 rather than, say, a .30-06, which would require a considerably larger safe zone. The warning on the side of the .22 ammo box indicating that the bullet will carry for a mile is correct. You should walk the perimeter of any area where you are considering doing this kind of informal practice.

Even though you might be shooting at pinecones or twigs on the ground or leaves floating in a stream, you must take care with every shot that there is no possibility of it going astray. In all cases, you must ensure that no person or living creature is in your line of fire, no matter how distant. Fire each shot as if it were your only shot, and be aware of its path. There is never any excuse for endangering others and certainly not for the sake of shooting practice.

In addition to targets of opportunity, such as pinecones, you can improve your marksmanship considerably by using informal targets, such as half-inflated balloons, tennis balls, and soft drink cans tied to low-hanging branches or placed on tree stumps or on the ground. Full soft drinks cans are more fun to shoot than empty ones, since they blow up with a satisfying spray.

I often have young or first-time shooters start by shooting a full soft drink can with a .22. Doing so engenders respect for the diminutive cartridge. Having the contents of the soft drink blow up and spray everything, then examining a blown-out can is a clear visual demonstration of the power of even the smallest caliber.

Low-speed .22 solid impacting a soft drink can. © Justin Ayres

High-speed .22 hollow point meets soft drink can.

Low-speed .22 solid meets orange.

High-speed .22 hollow point meets orange.

Since you are the kind of responsible person who would buy this book, you will, like all responsible shooters, pick up and pack out any debris, blown out cans, perforated balls, popped balloons, and so on. You don't want other shooters to mistake you for a careless, inconsiderate gun owner who uglifies the world by leaving empty ammo boxes and other debris lying around for others to clean up. Right?

RAPID FIRE

Once you can call your shots on bull's-eyes and informal targets and have done a reasonable amount of it—say, a couple of hundred rounds—

Further damage from when a high-speed .22 hollow point meets a soft drink can.

you are ready for rapid fire. Start the same way. Fire your first shot as if it were your only shot. Then, without a moment's pause, trigger your second shot. If you've done everything right, you will find two holes in your target so close together they might be touching.

The next method of rapid fire is to regain your sight picture and immediately fire another round. This is kind of moot with a .22 due to the lack of recoil—odds are you won't lose your sight picture.

Repeat the process to put more than two shots on target.

MOVING TARGETS

Half-filled balloons left to blow along the ground or float downstream make good moving targets. Unless you're in a hurricane or you've tossed those balloons into a raging river, they won't be moving too fast. Paper plates tied to branches and left to blow in the wind also work well.

Look at your target and bring your gun to bear so your sights come to the target. Then track the target as it moves and squeeze your round off as you continue to move with the target.

Tracking paper plate target.

Paper plates hanging from a tree.

Paper plates as informal targets. © Justin Ayres

PPK .22 and a student's target.

Glock 19 and a student's target.

THE FLINCH

I will deal with flinching at some length because of the reluctance of many people to actually discuss the issue, and because the most common cause for misses that I have observed is the anticipation of recoil and muzzle blast leading to jerking the trigger, pushing, pulling, or heeling, the handgun or shouldering the rifle or shotgun. All of these actions move the weapon out of alignment. (It is also the most common cause for new shooters to get discouraged and quit the sport.)

Few shooters, especially male shooters, will admit to a flinch. Flinching is the absolute bane of the shooter but is one of the most common causes for misses and the limiting factor in shooting powerful weapons. Female shooters seem to have no problem admitting to a flinch and therefore have less trouble overcoming one. It's difficult to cure something you deny exists. This is one of the key reasons, but far from the only one, that I advocate starting with the

.22. Flinches are caused by reacting to recoil and muzzle blast; the .22 has virtually none of either.

Among certain groups of shooters, the issue of the flinch is sort of a dirty little secret—something many have but no one wants to admit. This seems to be a uniquely American phenomenon. I have shot with men in other countries—experienced shooters, some of them professionals—who openly complained about the kick of a big gun and talked about how they were working to overcome their flinch.

Indeed, this is an important point of discussion among African Professional Hunters—men who hunt the largest and most dangerous game on earth. These men deal with large guns, such as the .500 Express, to ensure dropping large dangerous game in its tracks at close range during a charge.

Over drinks one night in a transit lounge in the Dubai airport, I talked with a professional hunter who had been at the game for more than twenty years. He told me that he took pains to make sure his clients were armed with a rifle they could shoot accurately. He was quite clear that he would rather have a client with a .30-06 shooting 220-grain solids who could place shots every time on a moving target the size of a playing card than a client who insisted on shooting a big double rifle he or she couldn't handle. In his view, it was part of the professional hunter's job to back up the client with a big gun. Few nonprofessionals can afford the investment of time and money to maintain proficiency with the big guns. As we talked further, I found that he was afflicted with severe arthritis and a fair amount of hearing loss—part of the price the big guns extract for mastery.

Even an ordinary .30-06 takes some work to get accustomed to for most people. When I was young, in military training, and still dumb enough to volunteer, I became the designated shooter to use up the extra ammo after the day's training was over. The other troops would load up on the back of the trucks and head for the barracks while I stayed at the range with one or two of the training sergeants until the ammo was all fired—or the sergeants got tired of hanging around.

The range had pop-ups and a jungle walk, as well as other entertaining attractions. I often burned up an extra two to three hundred rounds of .308 and would continue to shoot for an hour or so after dark when the sergeants didn't drag me away earlier. In truth, I welcomed the opportunity to improve skills I expected would be instrumental in my future survival. Sometimes I arrived back at the barracks after the mess hall had closed, which will give you some idea how serious I was about my shooting. Missing chow for an eighteen-year-old paratrooper was a *big* deal.

A couple of decades later, after not having occasion to fire a high-powered rifle for three or four years, I dusted off my old M1 Garand (chambered for the .30-06, the M1 was the predecessor to the M14 and was the rifle I learned in basic training) and went to the range. Have you ever seen an angry horse kick out with his hind leg? That was roughly comparable to the severity of my flinch. I was stunned. Who, me? I had a flinch? Yes! Sure did. It took me a couple of days to relax into that Garand again. I let that flinch go like the bad habit it was. But it can happen to anyone and with much less gun.

DIAGNOSING A FLINCH

The basic technique for diagnosing a flinch is to have a coach load a dummy round in your magazine without telling you which is the dummy round. When you squeeze the trigger on a dummy round, it will become immediately apparent if you have a flinch. The diagnosis is also part of the cure. Return to dry fire for about fifty rounds. Then, when you resume live fire, you will retain the memory of the dry fire. Do not anticipate the shot. Squeeze the trigger, let it happen, and relax into the shot. Have your coach again load a dummy round after you resume live fire. You should find that the flinch has been corrected. Most people flinch more from the muzzle blast, or the noise, than from the actual recoil. If you're still having a problem, upgrade your ear protection. Nine out of ten times that will do the trick.

Some people cannot get over a flinch induced by a powerful gun. In that event, simply choose a gun with less recoil. I am no great believer in power as the defining characteristic of any firearm. If the shooter cannot fire the gun accurately, the gun is basically useless except as a noisemaker.

CHAPTER 4

How to Shoot a Rifle

Fundamentals of marksmanship are the same for any rifle, in that rifles shoot a single projectile at high speed. The shotgun shoots multiple projectiles at slower speeds and those projectiles slow down much faster. Therefore, somewhat different methods are required for the shotgun. The handgun, lacking a shoulder stock, requires its own methods.

In other sections I distinguish between carbines and rifles, but practically speaking the basic shooting methods are the same.

BASIC RIFLE MARKSMANSHIP

As in chapter 3 on the fundamentals of marksmanship, the basics of shooting a rifle accurately are:

- Identify your target.
- Steady your position.
- Align the sighting system with the target.
- Fire without disturbing the alignment of the sights.

TARGET IDENTIFICATION

Observing and identifying your target is a simple matter when you're shooting bull's-eyes at a shooting range, but it is more difficult in the hunting or competition field. You must always be sure to aim at what you intend to shoot. Do not mistake Farmer Brown's cow for a deer. When you are sure of your target, start the aiming process.

STEADY POSITION

1. Foregrip: The foregrip rests in the non-firing hand, which is the left hand if you're right-handed. The forearm should be held firmly but lightly. The elbow should be under the forearm. This will enable a relaxed but steady position and allow the rifle to move freely to engage moving or multiple targets.

Foregrip illustrated.

2. Butt: The rifle butt is placed firmly into the hollow of the firing shoulder. This will aid in acquiring a steady position and minimize the effects of recoil. The trigger finger is placed so the rifle will not be disturbed when the trigger is squeezed. Rearward pressure with the remaining three fingers will aid in stabilizing the firing position and reducing recoil.

Rifle butt firmly in pocket of shoulder.

3. Cheek-to-Stock Weld: Your neck should be relaxed, allowing your cheek to be placed naturally on the stock. The stock weld must provide a natural line of sight through the center of the rear sight aperture, or notch, to the front sight post and on to the target. This alignment is critical. You may find that some rifles do not allow you to achieve a proper cheek-to-stock weld. If not, ask an experienced shooter to help you get fitted. Often a cheek pad will do the trick.

Showing cheek-to-stock weld.

4. Support: Correct body alignment will, as much as possible, use the bones to support the rifle. In field firing, if any fixed support, such as a tree, is available, it should be used. But the shooter must learn to support the rifle without a rest.

Bench rest.

5. Muscle Relaxation: When the correct position is attained, you should be able to relax into position and hold it for some time without muscle fatigue. This will probably require some practice to become fully comfortable.

Correct body alignment.

To become a marksman, a steady, consistent position with a solid cheek weld must be acquired and mastered to the point where it is reflexive when the rifle is brought to the shoulder. If these basics are in place, you can build on them and eventually be able to shoot quickly and accurately even under difficult conditions. The key is to develop a natural point of aim that will allow you to align your rifle and sights exactly with your target every time you shoulder your rifle.

ALIGNING THE SIGHT SYSTEM

1. Sight Alignment: To align your sights correctly, place the tip of the front sight in the center of the rear aperture or notch if using open sights.

Correct sight alignment and sight picture.

2. Focus: Focus your eye on the front sight. Doing so will naturally center the front sight in the rear sight, thus aligning them.

This causes the target to look slightly blurred, although the front sight will be in sharp focus. Every shooter must learn this fundamental technique. If your focus is on the front sight, only minor aiming errors should happen.

3. Sight Picture: A correct sight picture consists of the aiming point on the target, the front sight post, and the rear sight— all in alignment. If you have practiced the points above, a good sight picture should naturally form.

FIRING WITHOUT DISTURBING THE SIGHTS

BREATH CONTROL

Controlling the breath aids in maintaining stability and alignment while squeezing the trigger. There are two breath control techniques commonly used.

1. When there is sufficient time to allow natural respiration, you should squeeze the trigger after exhaling during the natural pause before inhaling.

2. If there is not enough time to allow for the previous technique, simply hold your breath at the moment you squeeze the trigger.

TRIGGER SQUEEZE

A proper trigger squeeze will fire the rifle without disturbing the alignment. A sudden movement (jerking) of the trigger will move the rifle out of alignment, causing a miss. A flinch will also move the rifle with the same result.

The index finger should be placed on the trigger so it touches between the first joint and the tip of the finger. Some prefer to place the pad of the first joint on the trigger; some prefer to use the area just behind the pad. Either will do if it works for you.

Correct finger position, ready to fire.
© ML Ayres

The trigger must be squeezed directly to the rear with a steady movement. In the beginning, care must be taken so that the squeeze is not off center. Pressing the trigger to one side or the other will result in pulling the shot out of alignment. When cultivating this skill, visualize pressing the trigger directly to the rear of the butt, as if a rod connects the butt and the trigger. In time, this will come naturally.

WOBBLE

Unless you are shooting from a solid rest, your sights will wobble somewhat, moving your sights away from your target and back to it. This is normal. If you have a strongly supported position, there will be little wobble. Do not try to anticipate the wobble by jerking the trigger. If your sights move off target during your squeeze, wait until they return to the target and resume your controlled squeeze.

Getting a good position, acquiring a proper sight picture, and executing a trigger squeeze may take an extended period of time for the beginning shooter. If you're totally new to shooting, you may take five or ten seconds just on the trigger squeeze, with the entire process consuming two or three minutes. With diligent practice, you will learn to perform this sequence in a split second. But first go slow, and don't concern yourself with speed.

SHOOTING POSITIONS

The above fundamentals apply regardless of the shooting position. However, a good, solid shooting position will improve your ability to hit. After mastering the fundamentals, you should be able to shoot from almost any position.

Note that in each position described and pictured, the alignment of the rifle and the sights are unchanged. The cheek-to-stock weld remains the same. The arms and hands are in the same positions. (I have listed the positions from first to last in the order I find them useful in the field, as opposed to range or competition.)

OFFHAND FIELD

The offhand field position is dynamic and relaxed. It is a position from which the shooter can see, shoot, and move with secure footing for field movement. If you have any experience with the martial arts, you will see that below the waist, the position amounts to a half horse.

Offhand Field 1.

Offhand Field 2.

Offhand Field 3.

Offhand Field 5.

SQUATTING

The squatting position is one of my favorites. It's lightning fast to drop into and step up from, both arms are supported, good accuracy is enabled, and it lowers your silhouette, which can be important in certain situations. Good lower back flexibility, indeed good general flexibility, will aid in assuming this position and making it comfortable. Dropping into this position and returning to a standing position amounts to a deep knee bend. If this position is a problem for you, try doing a couple dozen slow, deep knee bends a day for a week or so. Also, sitting

Offhand Field 4.

in this position, at first for short periods, will aid in flexibility. (The position will also keep your bottom dry when the ground is wet.)

Squatting.

SUPPORTED

If you are alert to your surroundings, you will often find something on which to rest your rifle. Whether shooting from a bench at a

Shooting from a bench rest 1.

Shooting from a bench rest 2.

Shooting from a bench rest 3.

range or taking a rest on a tree limb, supported positions provide maximum stability, thus, the best accuracy. Often you can find a position that offers both good support and good concealment. This is optimum when hunting, as it will help hide you from the ever-alert vision of your quarry.

KNEELING

Kneeling is an easily assumed position that is more stable than offhand, although less mobile.

The key in this position is to place the upper arm so that the fore elbow is forward of the knee. Some find this easier to assume than squatting.

OFFHAND TARGET

I distinguish between the two offhand positions because they are quite different in form and function. The designations, offhand target and offhand field, are my own. The offhand target position is a relaxed, erect standing position providing good stability with a good range of vision but with much less mobility than the field position.

Kneeling position 1.

Offhand target position 1.

Kneeling position 2.

Offhand target position 2.

Offhand target position 3.

Offhand target position 4.

Offhand target position 5.

SITTING

Slow to get into and out of, sitting is comfortable for long periods and gives both arms good support. In kneeling, one arm is supported. In sitting, you place the upper arms so that your elbows are in front of and supported by your knees; thus, both arms are supported.

Prone 1.

Prone 2.

Sitting with one arm supported.

PRONE

The prone position is the most stable of the unsupported positions. Actually, the position is well supported by the alignment of the body and its firm connection with the ground. Done correctly, the direct body-to-earth connection

Prone 3.

Prone 4.

forms a shooting platform that is as stable as a rest. As a field and hunting position, it excels where there is an open view and a long shot, such as you might encounter with plains game.

Standing (offhand target), sitting, kneeling, and prone are positions used in competition. The formal versions of these positions can be learned from an NRA instructor.

POINT SHOOTING OR SNAP SHOOTING

Point shooting or snap shooting, as it was called when I was a kid, has been pretty well understood since the invention of firearms. For some reason unknown to me, there is currently considerable controversy involving this shooting technique with various experts arguing that this basic skill does not work at all. Recently, I have heard convoluted arguments against the use of this technique, both for riflemen and hand gunners. Some younger but experienced shooters even tell me that such techniques belong in the realm of fantasy.

Point shooting or snap shooting now is known by a number of different names, but it amounts to the same thing: shooting without the use of sights. I'm not entirely sure how this controversy got started or what the point of it is. Perhaps it helps sell hobby magazines by the time-honored practice of setting up a straw man to knock down. Or possibly something has been lost during the development of the "new technique," which amounts to shooting fast with sights and both hands.

Back when our country was engaged in the Vietnam conflict, feedback from the combat zone was clear and unequivocal. The traditional marksmanship that was being taught to our troops wasn't doing the job in fast-breaking firefights, especially at close range and in poor lighting in brush. Something else was needed. The Army introduced a program called Quick Kill that used a Daisy BB gun without sights and various training aids and targets to teach snap shooting, also known as instinct or point shooting. BB guns were used because they made it safer to engage aerial targets and there was no recoil or muzzle blast to deal with, thereby freeing the trainee to focus on learning the skill. Later on, Daisy repackaged their air gun and training kit and marketed it to the public as Quick Skill.

The program worked quite well, with trainees quickly learning to hit targets (static then moving) without the aid of sights. They were even able to consistently hit candy wafers and coins when tossed into the air. I have heard some experts argue that in this type of shooting the shooter is unconsciously using the sights because there is no other way they could be getting these hits. Obviously these soldiers were not unconsciously using the sights, as there were no sights to be used. These skills served thousands of soldiers on the fields of battle and saved many American lives.

Forty years later, the military is still teaching Quick Kill, only now, according to current field manuals, they call it Reflexive Fire.

Before I was twelve, I learned to snap shoot fairly well with my .22. Heck, I had been doing it with a bow since I was five. From my personal experience, I thought the Army did a good job of teaching men who had never fired a gun how to shoot, both with and without sights. Instinct shooting, snap shooting, or whatever you want to call it has worked well for me, within its limits. Those limits are for me, with a rifle or carbine, about seventy-five yards. Others successfully snap shoot at longer distances. On more than one occasion, I have been obliged to shoot at moving targets at night. No sight picture was possible, yet I hit my targets. Thousands of others have done the same.

Later I was trained with a handgun using what our instructor called instinct shooting or shooting to live, which amounted to the same thing but using pistols instead of rifles. I'll deal with the use of this technique for handguns in

the section on self-defense. Here, I'll explain how it works for rifles. It is a valuable part of any shooter's skill set and well worth spending some time to learn.

No matter what you call it, the following is how to point or snap shoot a rifle.

1. Bring the rifle up to your shoulder and look down the barrel. Focus on your target, preferably a small part of your target, such as a letter on the logo of a soft drink can or a red spot on a bull's-eye. Squeeze the trigger.
2. The key is to look at your target, not your sights. The better your focus on the target; the better your hits will be.

If you've done your foundational work and have your body alignment grooved in, cheek-to-stock weld and so fourth, you'll find your sights are roughly lined up and you can consistently score hits on small paper plates out to about twenty-five yards without taking time to acquire a sight picture. With a little more practice, you can extend that range to about fifty to seventy-five yards. There are quite a number of people who can effectively snap shoot at much greater distances. Maybe you can also with good, tightly focused, concentrated practice. But just about anyone can reach the first level in a couple of days, assuming they have already learned basic gun handling.

If you would like to improve your skills in this area, practice with informal moving targets, as I mentioned earlier. If you find yourself looking for a sight picture while practicing snap shooting, try putting tape over your sights—that's what our sergeants had us do when we went to rifles.

If bow hunters can hit a small paper plate at twenty-five yards, and most of them can, you can certainly do the same with a rifle without sights. I've known more than one bow hunter who could, and did, hit birds on the wing, no sights used or needed. Give it a serious try before accepting anyone's word that it can't be done.

CHAPTER 5

How to Shoot a Handgun

HANDGUN FUNDAMENTALS

Some of the basics of rifle shooting also apply to handgun shooting. To shoot well, you need a solid grip, good trigger control, proper breathing, and when using the sights, a good sight picture (correct alignment of the sights with the target). However, you don't have a shoulder stock to stabilize your gun, only your shaky hands and arms. The handgun also lacks the long sight radius of the rifle, which magnifies mistakes in alignment. However, with good technique and practice,

most people can become proficient with the handgun.

It's important to realize that practical ranges with the handgun are much shorter than for the rifle. In the movies, it's common to see the hero point shooting and hitting the bad guy at fifty yards and more while he's running, uphill and downhill, on rooftops, or while driving at one hundred miles an hour. In real life, not so much. As with the rifle, aimed shooting with sights is foundational and the preferred technique for hitting targets at longer ranges. Formal bull's-eye target competition is done at distances to about twenty-five yards. Other kinds of competition utilize targets as far away as one hundred yards. Long range for handgun point shooting is anything farther than approximately seven yards, although this distance varies for each person. There are those who can reliably hit their target point shooting over longer distances.

With a good grounding in aimed shooting with sights, you could possibly take to the field as a handgun hunter, although I recommend also gaining proficiency in snap shooting before going afield. If you choose to hunt with your handgun, you should limit the range of your shot at any game animal to that which you are certain you can hit reliably. For, a squirrel or rabbit, your effective target is no larger than a teacup; for a deer, it is the size of a small paper plate.

In handgun shooting you will apply the fundamentals of rifle shooting, albeit modified to fit the handgun.

- Identify your target.
- Steady position.
- Align the sighting system with the target.
- Fire without disturbing the alignment of the sights.

IDENTIFY YOUR TARGET

Identifying your target is as important when shooting a handgun as with a rifle. Given that effective handgun distances are shorter than rifle distances, it should be easy to correctly identify your target—unless you're under the stress of self-defense.

STEADY POSITION – GRIP

The handgun shooting grip is as important to the pistol as the shoulder position and cheek weld is to rifle shooting. Ideally, the handgun becomes an extension of the hand and arm. With a firm, uniform, consistent grip, the handgun can point as well as your index finger.

Correct grip.

ONE-HANDED GRIP

Grasp the handgun with the V formed by the thumb and index finger. This V should be placed as high as possible on the back of the grip and in alignment with the barrel and sights. Wrap your lower three fingers around the grip and grasp firmly, placing strong pressure primarily toward the rear of the grip. Too much sideways pressure from the fingers can torque the gun out of align-

Grip the pistol so it is in line with the arm.

ment and lead to missing your target. A firm grip is critical in virtually all handgun shooting, with the exception of formal bull's-eye target shooting where a more relaxed grip is commonly used. The index finger is placed above the trigger on the frame, unless you are drawing to fire at once.

TWO-HANDED GRIP

The two-handed grip, correctly applied, provides more support and stability for the firing hand. Close the fingers of the nonfiring hand over the firing hand with the nonfiring fingers placed in the grooves between the fingers of the firing hand. Apply firm pressure to obtain maximum stability.

Some favor the push–pull method to aid in recoil control, applying forward pressure with the firing hand and backward pressure with the nonfiring hand. Others prefer an all-around firm grip. You will need to do a bit of experimentation to determine which works for you. Never allow the nonfiring hand to pull the firing hand out of alignment. Be sure to maintain full grip pressure with the firing hand.

Two-handed field grip 2.

Two-handed field grip 1.

Two-handed field grip 3.

Two-handed field grip 4.

Two-handed field grip 5.

ALIGNING THE SIGHT SYSTEM WITH THE TARGET

SIGHT ALIGNMENT

Few handguns use an aperture sight, although some are fitted with a ghost ring a large aperture.

Most common is the square notch sight. To align this sight, place the front blade into the rear notch. The top of the front sight should be level with the top of the rear sight and centered in the rear notch.

Aligning the sight.

FOCUS

Focus your eye on the front sight. Doing so will naturally center the front sight in the rear sight, thus aligning them. This causes the target to look slightly blurred, although the front sight will be in sharp focus. Every shooter must learn this fundamental technique. If your focus is on the front sight, only minor aiming errors should happen.

SIGHT PICTURE

A correct sight picture consists of the aiming point on the target, the front sight post, and the rear sight—all in alignment. If you have practiced the points above, a good sight picture should naturally form. The eye cannot focus on the front sight, rear sight, and target. Focusing on the front sight is most conducive to accuracy. The best way to do this is to look through the rear sight and focus on the front sight when it is placed over your target.

Front sight on target, rear sights blurred.

FIRING WITHOUT DISTURBING ALIGNMENT

BREATH CONTROL

There are two breath control techniques commonly used.

1. When there is sufficient time to allow natural respiration, you should squeeze the trigger after exhaling during the natural pause before inhaling.
2. If there is not enough time to allow for the previous technique, simply hold your breath at the moment you squeeze the trigger.

TRIGGER SQUEEZE

A proper trigger squeeze is even more critical in handgun shooting than in rifle work. A sudden movement or jerking of the trigger will move the handgun out of alignment to the extent that a shooter can miss a life-sized silhouette target from five feet. In my experience, the most common cause for jerking the trigger is a flinch.

The index finger should be placed on the trigger so it touches between the first joint and the tip of the finger. Some prefer to place the pad of the first joint on the trigger; some prefer to use the area just behind the pad. Either will do if it works for you.

The trigger must be squeezed directly to the rear with a steady movement. In the beginning, care must be taken so the squeeze is not off center. Pressing the trigger to one side or the other can torque the handgun out of alignment. When forming this skill, visualize pressing the trigger directly to the rear of the butt, as if a rod connects the trigger, the back of the grip, and your forearm. In time this will come naturally. Dry firing is probably the most important practice to ensure you are squeezing the trigger properly.

If you are using a double-action automatic, the trigger pull will be greater and require more pressure than subsequent single-action shots,

Index finger placed on trigger.

perhaps twice as much. Extra attention should be used to master double-action fire. In double-action revolvers, all shots are double-action unless the revolver is manually cocked.

WOBBLE

The wobble effect that the rifle shooter experiences will be more pronounced with the handgun. You should do your best to control wobble with proper breathing, grip, and trigger control.

SHOOTING POSITIONS

Handgun shooting positions are similar in form and function to the rifle positions. All provide greater stability than the offhand positions. Utilized properly and with the right pistol, you can get amazing accuracy. Some years ago, I knew shooters who were enamored with the 9mm Sig 210, understandably so. The Sig 210 was once the Swiss Army's issue sidearm and easily the most accurate service pistol on the planet. These fellows considered it great fun to haze a coffee can back and forth at a hundred yards. Like them, I found a coffee can to be an easy target at a hundred yards using this pistol. By shooting from one of the positions described here, we could toss a coffee can around at farther than a hundred yards. I won't strain your credulity with the actual distances. Learn offhand first. Then try the positions below. You might be surprised.

FIELD POSITION

In the rifle section, I called this position the offhand field position. For the pistol, I'll call it the field position. It is basically the same as the rifle position from the waist down, and it is equally important in order to have a solid base from which to fire. Lacking the rifle's shoulder stock, a stable hold is dependent on correct alignment of the shoulders and arms. This is an especially important position in that you will likely do most of your handgun shooting from it. It is a dynamic and powerful position from which the shooter can see, shoot, and move with secure footing over broken ground.

As the photos on page 44 show, a one- or two-handed grip can be used in the field position.

SUPPORTED

Taking a rest is a good practice with rifle or handgun, especially so with the handgun. A tree limb, or any solid object, will enable you to have an almost unwavering sight picture and resultant accuracy.

PRONE

As with the rifle, prone is the most stable handgun position other than shooting from a rest.

Prone 1.

Prone 2.

Prone 3.

Prone 4.

SQUATTING

The squatting position works well in the field, as it is quick to assume and offers good stability.

Squatting.

KNEELING

The kneeling position offers less stability than squatting for some shooters and more stability for others. The comparative utility of the two positions is determined by the individual's physical make up.

Kneeling.

POINT SHOOTING OR SNAP SHOOTING

I cover point or snap shooting in some detail in chapter 4 on rifle shooting. For the handgun, the primary difference is that you do not have the stability provided by the rifle's shoulder stock. However, within the limits of the handgun, this method works equally well.

Starting with your gun hand at your side and a firm grip on the handgun, bring your gun hand up with your arm fully extended toward your target. You may use only one hand, or you can bring your other hand up and grasp your gun hand to better stabilize your handgun. Look down the barrel. Focus on your target, preferably a small part of your target. Squeeze the trigger.

The key is to look at your target, not your sights. The better your focus on the target, the better your hits will be.

Focus on the target, not the sights.

Please review chapter 15, "Guns for Self-Defense," for more detailed information regarding handguns and the point shooting method.

DRY FIRING FOR THE HANDGUN

Dedicated and concentrated dry fire practice is vitally important to learning the handgun and maintaining skill. An intensively concentrated half hour of practice in the evening is something you can do anywhere you have your firearm—no range or ammo required. Once skills are acquired, much less practice is needed to maintain them.

If your dry fire practice is to be of maximum benefit, it is critical to practice as if you were shooting a loaded gun. First, make absolutely sure your gun is unloaded. Then put the ammunition away in a drawer or if traveling, perhaps in your case. Then put yourself in the frame of mind you would be in if you were shooting under actual field conditions. Shoot fifty imaginary rounds with full concentration. Balancing a coin on the barrel of your gun for the first five rounds and the last five rounds is an excellent way to see if you are jerking the trigger or in any way not squeezing off your imaginary rounds correctly.

I have experienced extended periods, usually while traveling internationally, when I had no access to shooting facilities. I have found that during those periods, I was able to maintain my skills by two simple exercises. One was a few minutes of dry fire in the privacy of my hotel room perhaps once a week, preferably just before retiring for the night.

Any skill practiced immediately before sleep will take on a sort of momentum effect as if you had continued to practice while sleeping. The second was to visualize a perfect shot after getting in bed just before sleep. Visualization is a key technique to improving your skills. I will discuss this in more detail in chapter 7, "The Tao of Shooting." If the reader would like to go more deeply into this subject, read my book *The Tao of Survival.*

CHAPTER 6

How to Shoot a Shotgun

Since a shotgun possesses only a front sight (unless set up for slugs, in which case it is fired as a rifle), there is no point to separating shooting techniques into aimed with sights and aimed without sights, or point shooting, instinct shooting, or any of the other designations. All shotgun shooting amounts to point shooting.

Shotgun. © Remington

The basic method of mounting the shotgun to the shoulder is the same as for the rifle. The most effective shooting position is what I refer to as the offhand field position. The offhand target position lacks the needed stability. Since shotguns are most commonly used for wing shooting, there is no need to consider the other shooting positions.

OFFHAND FIELD

The offhand field position is dynamic and relaxed. It is a position from which the shooter can see, shoot, and move with secure footing for field movement. If you have any experience with the martial arts, you will see that below the waist the position amounts to a half horse. The position is illustrated in photos on the next page (although it shows the shooter with a rifle, there is no difference in application). See chapter 4 on rifles for more images of proper long gun techniques.

Let's assume you're shooting at a moving target, clay, pheasant, quail, or other flying bird. As in the rifle or handgun, look first at your target and bring the gun to the target. Look down the barrel and swing your shotgun to follow the target. Lead your target to allow for the load you are using and squeeze the trigger. You must know your load and where it shoots to be successful. You will learn this with practice. Since the projectiles of a shotgun travel much more slowly than those of a rifle or even a handgun, you cannot aim directly at a fast moving target. Instead, you must aim in front of your target and continue to move as you squeeze the trigger, thus stringing, or placing, your shot pattern where your target will be. You must also know the pattern your shotgun shoots with the load you are using. Each load will pattern somewhat differently.

In shotgun shooting, you must apply most of the fundamentals of rifle shooting, albeit somewhat modified.

- Identify your target.
- Steady position.
- Align the sighting system with the target.
- Fire without disturbing the alignment of the sights.

IDENTIFY YOUR TARGET

Identifying your target is a simple matter when you're shooting clays at a shooting range but somewhat more difficult in the hunting field. However, you must ensure that you are aiming at what you think you are shooting. Do not mistake Farmer Brown's prized turkeys for pheasants.

STEADY POSITION

FOREGRIP

The foregrip rests in the nonfiring hand (the left hand if you're right-handed). The forearm should be held firmly but lightly. The elbow should be under the forearm. This will enable a relaxed but steady position and allow the shotgun to move freely to engage moving or multiple targets.

BUTT

The shotgun butt is placed firmly into the hollow of the firing shoulder. This will aid in acquiring a steady position and minimize the effects of recoil. The trigger finger is placed so the shotgun will not be disturbed when the

Offhand field position, demonstrated with rifle.

trigger is squeezed. A slight rearward pressure with the remaining three fingers will aid in stabilizing the firing position and reducing recoil.

CHEEK-TO-STOCK WELD

Your neck should be relaxed, allowing your cheek to be placed naturally on the stock. The stock weld must provide a natural line of sight along the barrel to the front sight and on to the target.

SUPPORT

Correct body alignment will, as much as possible, use the bones to support the shotgun.

MUSCLE RELAXATION

When the correct position is attained, you should be able to relax into position and hold it for some time without muscle fatigue.

A steady, consistent position with a solid cheek weld must be acquired and mastered to the point where it is reflexive when the shotgun is brought to the shoulder. If these basics are in place, you can build on them and eventually be able to shoot quickly and accurately even under difficult conditions. The key is to develop a natural point of aim that will allow you to align your shotgun with your target every time you shoulder your shotgun.

ALIGNING THE SIGHT SYSTEM

For the shotgun, aligning the sighting system amounts to looking down the barrel to the front sight. Although this is simpler than aligning the rear sight and front sight of a rifle, it is no less critical.

FIRING WITHOUT DISTURBING SIGHT ALIGNMENT

BREATH CONTROL

Controlling the breath aids in maintaining stability and alignment while squeezing the trigger. There are two breath control techniques commonly used:

1. When there is sufficient time to allow natural respiration, you should squeeze the trigger after exhaling during the natural pause before inhaling.
2. If there is not enough time to allow for the previous technique, simply hold your breath at the moment you squeeze the trigger.

TRIGGER SQUEEZE

A proper trigger squeeze will fire the shotgun without disturbing the alignment. A sudden movement or jerking of the trigger will move the shotgun out of alignment, causing a miss. A flinch will also move the shotgun with the same result.

The index finger should be placed on the trigger so it touches between the first joint and the tip of the finger. Some prefer to place the pad of the first joint on the trigger; some prefer to use the area just behind the pad. Either will do if it works for you.

The trigger must be squeezed directly to the rear with a steady movement. In the beginning, care must be taken so that the squeeze is not off center. Pressing the trigger to one side or the other will result in pulling the shot out of alignment. When forming this skill, visualize pressing the trigger directly to the rear of the butt, as if a rod connects the butt and the trigger. In time this will come naturally.

FIELDS OF FIRE

Understanding fields of fire is of maximum importance when upland shooting with companions. When shooters form up to cross a field or make a firing line, they will set out individual fields of fire in accordance with the shooters on each side of them. Generally, each shooter's field of fire will extend from his position in an imaginary cone downrange, perhaps slightly overlapping his companion's range to either side of the fields of fire. Once established, fields of fire should be maintained and not transgressed in the excitement of shooting.

TOO MUCH GUN

Perhaps even more so than with rifles and handguns, many people have a tendency to try to shoot more gun than they can handle when using a shotgun. This is always a mistake. I have seen fine wing shooting by men and women with light 28-gauge shotguns. Their take of birds fully equaled that of their more heavily armed companions, who were shooting the standard 12-gauge.

One day at a sporting clay range, I saw a man trying to teach his young wife to shoot a 12-gauge semiautomatic shotgun. The woman was a good sport, but she weighed maybe one hundred pounds and had obviously been given no instruction on how to hold a shotgun to absorb recoil. Each time she fired, the stock slapped her cheek and the butt slammed her shoulder, moving her back a couple of steps. It was painful to watch but certainly not as painful as what this young woman was enduring.

I noticed that the report of their guns was much louder than that of my gun or those of my companions. When they moved ahead a station I examined one of her expended shells. She was shooting high-base three-inch magnums. This is a round suitable for ducks and geese and grossly inappropriate for clays. In addition to throwing a pattern that makes it harder to score a hit on clays, the round kicks like a mule. The woman certainly had gumption, but I doubt her husband will ever get her to the range again. Maybe that was his purpose. Maybe he wanted some time alone or with the guys. But if he wanted a shooting companion, he lost her that day.

CHAPTER 7

The Tao of Shooting

Tao means "way," nothing more, nothing less. Taoist directed attention, which I am going to briefly discuss, has nothing to do with religion. It is a method or way of focusing attention to improve performance and a discipline practiced by Asian warriors, hunters, and sages for centuries. The methods used for shooting and other skills are similar to those used by Native American hunters, shamans, and warriors, and First Peoples from the Artic to the Amazon. Today certain elite military units and covert action groups practice these techniques.

I have seen bowmen, users of various primitive projectile weapons, and champion competitive shooters who use exactly these methods. Perhaps most importantly, I have seen these methods used in firefights by combat survivors. I have trained in and studied these methods for decades, use them myself, and have written extensively about them. For those who are interested in expanding their skills and knowledge, I provide detailed training methods in my book, *The Tao of Survival.*

I suspect all cultures that lived close to the earth once knew these methods, but our European ancestors forgot about them long ago. We gained a great deal with the age of reason, but some things were also lost. We are fortunate that Asian cultures codified and passed those methods down to us. These skills are enjoying a renaissance and today are practiced by many world-class athletes, not only martial artists and competitive shooters, but golfers, tennis players, track stars, and ball players of all kinds. Such well-known teams as the Oakland Raiders employ these methods. There is nothing foofoo, silly, or religous about the Tao.

After learning basic methods and disciplines, you can, by using focused attention, integrate those skills into your reflexes so you do the correct thing without consciously thinking about it. I first came to formal study of the Tao through martial arts. It was only after I had trained for some time that I realized that I had been using certain Taoist techniques for years without being aware of it. This is true for many others.

When I first qualified for the 82nd Airborne Division's pistol team, I was exhausted at the end of each day by the concentration required to meet and maintain the team standard. I worked so hard and concentrated so intensely that I dreamed of bull's-eyes with ten shots centered in them. Although I did not know it at the time, this is actually a formal technique called visualization.

After about a week of daily shooting, I discovered that I did better when I focused intensely just at the moment of firing and relaxing when I was off the trigger. After some more time, I learned to get the same results when I was relaxed. This is Taoist method in its essence.

First learn your foundation skills; nothing can replace them. Learn them well. Take your time and go step by step. Skip nothing.

FIRST EXERCISE

Find a quiet and comfortable spot. Sit in whatever position is comfortable for you. You do not have to get into a Lotus or even cross your legs. An easy chair will do just fine.

Let all thoughts of your day slip away. Don't fight with yourself, tell yourself to think of nothing, or try to force your thoughts to go away. It's okay if you find yourself reliving that moment when a truck cut you off on the freeway. Just don't dwell on the moment. Let that thought and all other thoughts slip away like bubbles in a stream.

Now recreate the feelings in your body when everything was correctly aligned and you made the perfect shot. Really *feel* in your body the muscle memory of your rifle or handgun.

Feel the stock against your shoulder, the grips in your hand, and the trigger under your finger. Remember, relive, and *feel* that moment when you made that perfect shot—the best shot of the day—the best shot of the week—the best shot ever. The more attention you put into this inner vision, the better your results will be.

SECOND EXERCISE

Once you have felt your body position in fine detail, visualize your sight picture over your target. Really *see* the target. Remember the best shot you've made on that target. Once you can see the target, *see* your bullet flying straight to your target, as if it's on a wire being pulled to the target.

You will be distracted. Don't be discouraged. Like any skill, this takes time to acquire. When you lose your concentration, just relax and let it go for a moment; gently move your attention back and recreate the first or second exercise.

These two exercises can be done separately or sequentially. Doing them at night before sleep will help focus your unconscious and get it to work for you.

THIRD EXERCISE

Go to your safe shooting spot, the familiar one where you have been shooting. The one where there is no possibility of anyone being downrange. Set up one target. Go to your shooting position; look at your target and focus your attention on it. *See* it in detail.

For this training to be successful, you must focus with intensity on your target. Do not think about the drive to your shooting spot, the weather, or the fly buzzing around your nose. Let all of those thoughts drift away like bubbles in a stream. Don't think. Just do. Fire without thinking about each step in the process. Shoot three shots and check your group. If you've done all the steps, or even most of them, you'll have a good group. Repeat the exercise.

Just as when you begin to do martial arts, ride a bicycle, or drive a car, you have to consciously learn the basics. In martial arts, you stand and move consciously and thoughtfully in a classic horse for hours and days and repeat basic techniques many times. But once you have them grooved in, you don't have to think about doing them. When you snap out a punch you don't think, horse position, hip rotation, snap, etc. But it's there because of the hours you invested in training. So too with the fundamentals of shooting.

Training in this way and using these steps can be a shortcut to shooting mastery. If you find a moment of stillness within yourself at the moment you squeeze your trigger and learn to focus all your attention for just one fraction of a second, you will have taken a giant step toward shooting mastery. There is more. But this is foundational and all we can go into in this book. These exercises will help to get skill foundations into your subconscious and muscle memory, both of which are much faster and surer than your conscious reasoning mind. If you find that you would like more information on this training read my book, *The Tao of Survival.*

CHAPTER 8

Hunting with Your Gun

Here's the most important thing to know about guns and hunting: **the shooter determines success of the hunt, not the gun**. Many books about guns for hunting go into deep, detailed discussion and analysis regarding caliber, load, gun models, scopes, and so forth. This is not that type of book. In this chapter, I will discuss some hunting methods, mention some recommended guns, and help you to select a gun that's right for you and the game you pursue.

If you know what you're doing, almost any decent gun will do. It's vitally important to keep this in mind. Do not fall into the trap of buying a rack of firearms in an attempt to compensate for lack of hunting success. If you enjoy firearm collecting, by all means build your collection, but be aware that collecting has little or nothing to do with hunting. As you progress in the sport, you may wish to expand your knowledge of various calibers and their performance; but to be a successful hunter, make sure you've got the basics down first.

Also, as a hunter you have an ethical obligation to acquire competency in shooting under field conditions. Ethical hunters reduce their game to possession by inflicting as little pain and suffering on their quarry as possible. The ideal is the clean shot—the unwary animal that drops without knowing what hit him. This ideal is not always achieved, but it should be attempted. We are, after all, sporting hunters. We hunt, for the most part, by choice, not by necessity. I have hunted with subsistence hunters in various places, including Asia and Latin America, and have found that they have their own methods that are useful to know if faced with survival conditions, but have no part in sporting hunting.

I have witnessed so-called hunters driving on fire roads in 4x4 trucks with racks of lights, the shooters standing in the truck bed ready to shoot the first deer they see. Don't do this. Don't be any part of it. It's illegal. It isn't sporting. It's just plain wrong. If you're caught spotlighting, you'll be arrested. If you're not caught, you'll know you have earned the contempt of all true hunters.

HUNTING BIG GAME

Current conventional wisdom has it that only extremely powerful large caliber rifles are suitable for large game. Yet, each year thousands of deer, elk, moose, and bear are taken with bows. Yes, I'm familiar with the argument that arrows kill by cutting vital organs and causing bleeding and that guns kill by shock, tissue destruction, or neural interruption. In this model, the razor-sharp arrow is superior to the bullet in causing blood wounds, but I don't think it's so simple. I've hunted successfully with both bow and gun and seen the results of many other hunters. I've witnessed deer run hundreds of yards before finally bleeding out and dropping after taking a lung shot from a high-powered rifle. I've seen virtually the same thing occur with an arrow-shot buck.

My observations and experience indicate that it's the accurate placement of the arrow or the bullet in a vital spot that gets the job done, rather than an excessively powerful rifle. Generally speaking, the best placement on large game is in the heart or lungs. Head and spine shots, being smaller targets, are more difficult and should only be taken if you know you can make the shot.

Many gun hunters would do well to emulate the bow hunter and get closer to their quarry to make sure they hit a vital spot. All too many hunters try to substitute power for marksmanship and shot placement. I hate to see a gut-shot deer, as does any hunter with respect for the animals he hunts. A new hunter might do well to try bow hunting. Experience with primitive weapons sharpens hunting skills. It also leads to a better appreciation of modern firearms.

I recently observed an instructor, who was teaching a state-approved safety class for first-time hunters, advise his students to choose nothing less than a .308 to take their first deer. By a show of hands, most of them had never even hunted rabbits. This occurred in a state where the average buck isn't much larger than my neighbor's German Shepherd. He went on to say that a .338 Winchester Magnum, or something more powerful, was the only chance the students would have to anchor a Colorado elk, given the enormous size and legendary hardiness of the elk. This is nonsense. This kind of advice has a good chance of driving a new hunter away from the sport. By all means use enough gun, but no more than you can handle or is appropriate for the game.

As my sons frequently remind me, I'm an old-school guy. I don't think a new hunter has much business going after large game until he or she has built a foundation of experience on small game. I also believe a new hunter needs a solid foundation of marksmanship and to develop a close familiarity with his or her weapon of choice. In addition, I do not think one has any business taking to the field without at least a rudimentary understanding of the habits and habitat of his intended quarry. Careful reading can help the new gun owner identify customary and successful methods for hunting. Learning from experienced hunters can be beneficial, if you're fortunate enough to find a good hunter to teach you.

Many years ago, I was hunting for deer and elk on a combination tag in Colorado with two friends and a local contact, George. One of my friends, Dexter, was outfitted with a beautiful new rifle. As I recall, it was a Remington 700 BDL chambered for the .300 Winchester Magnum and mounted with a good quality variable scope.

Remington Model 700 BDL. © Remington

Bob and I were somewhat envious of his rifle and the rest of his gear. We were both still in college; funds were limited and our guns and gear were considerably more modest. Bob carried an ancient Springfield Model 1903 with a sporterized stock his father had installed when it had been his rifle forty years previously. The old Springfield sported its original aperture, or peep, sight and its original chambering: .30-06. The stock displayed the nicks and dings of four decades of use. But the bore was bright and shiny, there was no rust anywhere on it, and it was well oiled. Of major importance, Bob shot his rifle regularly, was familiar with it from years of use, and had spent a few days at the range zeroing it with the ammunition he had selected for this hunt. He knew where his rifle would shoot with this particular load.

I wanted to try handgun hunting and had brought my duty revolver, a Smith & Wesson Model 19 .357 Magnum with a four-inch barrel. I had fired thousands of rounds with a half-dozen different loads with this revolver. The Smith was superbly accurate. I could shoot two-inch groups at fifty yards, hit the skittering balloons floating along the ground, and so on. Further, I planned to shoot within my limits. I had no intention of trying, say, a hundred-fifty-yard shot.

Smith & Wesson Model 19 .357 Magnum.

Dexter and George didn't think much of Bob's chances at an elk. They were of the opinion that the .30-06 was severely underpowered and incapable of dropping a monster elk. They also thought that without a scope he didn't have a chance, because he couldn't get close enough to bag an elk in the high country; maybe he'd get a deer down in the trees if he were lucky. As for me, I was beneath consideration. Everyone knew you couldn't hit an elk with a handgun, let alone put one down.

On our first day, just after dawn, about twenty miles down a logging road we saw a herd of elk in the middle of a meadow or park, as meadows are called in Colorado. All of us were out of the Land Cruiser in a flash and moved a hundred yards or so from the car, which as I recall, was about the minimum legal distance. It is not legal or sporting to shoot from or near a car.

BLAM! Dexter's muzzle was to my immediate left about fifteen feet away. He had fired without warning. Ears ringing, I moved back a few yards, as did Bob. Dexter fired again. BLAM! This time I was watching Dexter and saw him stagger backward from the recoil and poor footing. I watched, surprised as the elk totally ignored us. None of them went down. None of them even bothered to run. I had never before seen an elk herd and was amazed they had not all scrambled for cover at the first sight of us. Dexter fired another full magazine from his sitting position without hitting anything other than trees. No one else fired a shot. I think we were all stunned by the display of firepower and the lack of result.

We talked around the campfire that night, and Dexter admitted he had only fired one magazine from his new rifle before leaving California. He finally admitted that the rifle kicked him so bad when he had tried to zero it from a bench that he had given up and hoped to get a hit on his first shot or two. He showed us his bruised and purple shoulder by the light of our campfire, but there was no sympathy to be had from anyone.

Dexter made a number of errors, one of which was to fire before alerting us of his intention to do so. My ears were still ringing. I gave some thought to offering Dexter some vigorous instruction on field shooting protocol, aided by a chunk of firewood that was close at hand. (Zen masters frequently offer this type of physical instruction with the aid of what, in the Zendo, is called an encouragement stick.) Upon reflection, I decided a gentler approach might better serve, especially considering we were to spend the next week in camp together. So, I contented myself with some modest suggestions regarding behavior during the upcoming week.

However, his first error, made long before reaching our hunting grounds, had been to select a rifle that was beyond his ability to handle. His next mistake was failing to get enough practice with the big magnum to master it or at least zero it. He would have done better to select a more modest caliber, but Dexter had been seduced by the myth of the invincible elk.

Thousands of hunters annually make the same mistakes. Quite a few deer hunters are in the woods or mountains on opening day with a rifle they haven't fired since the year before, even to check zero. Others venture fourth with the newest magnum advertised to anchor that elk or deer. Few of them bring home any venison.

We fanned out after that first day and hunted separate meadows and ridges over the next week. Bob took his first elk cleanly with a nice ninety-yard (we paced it off) shot. George filled his deer tag by gut-shooting a doe at about three hundred yards and finishing her off with another three or four rounds. Dexter went the whole week without getting a hit on anything that moved.

Bob also filled his deer tag, so there was plenty of meat for all. And me? I bagged a six-point elk at about twenty yards. I put one round behind his ear and he dropped like, well, a few hundred pounds of meat. Anyone could have made that shot—anyone with rudimentary shooting skills and certainly anyone who had spent as much time working with that revolver as I had. The .357 pistol isn't as powerful as even the .223 rifle, but it was powerful enough to do what I asked of it.

Most big game hunting methods can be divided into stand hunting or stalking. Stand hunting is just what it sounds like: you wait for the game to come to you, sometimes in a natural stand, other times in man-made stands. Sometimes you do this after scouting out the land and the game, as in the elk hunt I just described. Sometimes, hunters travel to an unfamiliar area and are taken to stands by local guides. Still others set up their own stands, such as tree stands or devices that are fixed above the game's line of sight, where the hunter waits for the game to come by.

Then, there's stalking. On one of my best ever hunts, I spent three days in reconnaissance of a two-mile wide basin in the Northern California High Sierra. A necklace of small lakes and ponds was strung across the lush bottom, and short yellow grass grew in the soft ground around the ponds. Granite pushed its way out from the basins' slopes, and stands of pines and white barked trees grew between the cold stone outcrops.

I had spotted a small herd of mulies (hornless deer) at first light the day I arrived at the trailhead. I had also spotted a large group of hunters camped at the trailhead, who evidently did not see the herd I had spotted. They appeared to be too busy with bacon and coffee to look up. I had come to hunt, not to socialize, so instead of camping near the others, I moved off about 500 meters and spent some time watching the basin and slopes from a thick stand of pines. I made no fixed camp. I slept without a fire and ate cold food while I quietly scouted the area and waited for the hunters to leave, which they did the second day with much shouting and slamming of truck doors and no deer.

Then, over an afternoon and evening, I moved quietly and slowly around the outside of the basin to a spot just below the ridgeline. I spent the night rolled in my sleeping bag next to a leaf pile. I woke at first light and lay in my sleeping bag, watching first pale then golden light wash over the mountains. I waited until the sun was full in the sky, as I figured the mulies would be back in their beds from their browse.

Then I eased over the ridgeline and soft-footed slowly, slowly, slowly down the slope, the morning air currents still rising to meet me and carry my scent away from the herd's bedding ground in the center thickness of a golden leafed stand of aspens. It was no more than a half-mile from the closest pond on the floor of the basin. The morning breeze moved the leaves in their distinctive quaking motions and created a soft susurrus that masked what little noise I may have made.

They didn't even know I was there. The right thing to do might have been to take the shot that was offered. But I didn't have the heart to shoot one of them in its bed. I cleared my throat with a raspy sound that in retrospect might have sounded a little like a cougar or maybe just a man with a bit of congestion. They all jumped up as if they were on springs, and I dropped a small buck at about fifteen yards with a full-on chest shot that stopped his heart before he hit the ground.

You might want to try this kind of hunting. To me it's more satisfying than any other kind. There is not a thing in the world wrong with long-range hunting, and my hat is off to the marksman who makes those three-hundred-yard shots. Anyone who thinks his seven power scope and his .300 Winchester Magnum will make collecting that elk on the other side of that meadow an easy task hasn't been paying attention. Like I said, it's really just a matter of style. The long-range marksman often works just as hard for his game as that sneaky fellow crawling through the mud. And I think the work of it matters.

It seems to me that I should have to work hard before bringing death to my quarry. Somehow it changes the quality and texture of the whole experience and helps bring a measure of respect to the animal, which will become part of my family and me. You are what you eat. Literally. If I don't earn it, I might as well go buy a chunk of New Zealand venison and have done with it.

SMALL GAME

Rabbit, squirrels, and such are generally considered small game. In most jurisdictions, they can be legally taken with .22s or shotguns. Hunting small game can be at least as challenging as large game and often requires more shooting skill. It can also be rewarding.

I remember a long ago fall day about a week before school resumed, when I would once again be stuck in overheated rooms with black-boards and teachers with yard-long rulers, with which they were all too eager to correct errant behavior. I was eleven. I spent the better part of a crisp autumn afternoon crawling slowly and silently through dry, crunchy leaves, then sliding through foot-high river grass to get to a spot where I could get a good shot on a wary old groundhog. I probably should have taken another member of his tribe and left him to live out his remaining days with his brood, but I didn't. I did keep his skin and cook him over my campfire, the last one of the year. Groundhogs are considered varmints, but I wasted none of him, tough and gamy as he was. As have many young boys, I learned a great deal about stalking and hunting while after small game—knowledge and experience that served me well later on.

VARMINTS

Coyotes, groundhogs, ground squirrels, and prairie dogs are, generally speaking, not protected by law and are legal to take by various methods in various states. Check your local fish and game authority to make sure. In the West, many prairie dog hunters set up at long range from a dog town with a flat-shooting, scoped rifle and a spotting scope.

An outdoorsman I know practices for deer season by stalking marmots with a .22. He won't take a shot farther than fifteen to twenty yards. If you've ever been around marmots, you'll know how difficult it is to get that close.

In certain areas, coyotes have become a menace to domestic pets and small children. This is mainly due to loss of habitat. I've seen many coyotes taken with the .22. The .223 is also a good coyote cartridge, allowing more range and having much more effect. Many coyote hunters prefer the .243 or even the .270. There is a wide range of newer cartridges, some of which you may prefer.

WATERFOWL

There are places in Latin America where Native Americans hunt ducks by wearing helmets on their heads designed to look like their quarry, which allows them to wade or swim among the flocks resting on the water. They then grab a bird by its feet, pull it underwater—sort of like picking apples—and wring its neck. Then the bird is stuffed into an underwater basket worn around the waist and the hunter goes on to his next selection. This is not how ducks are commonly hunted here in the United States.

We usually use 12-gauge shotguns with number 2 to number 4 shot and shoot the bird while in flight, or at least we try to do so. Usually as the bird is coming in to land on water, ideally where the hunter has cleverly placed his or her decoys to attract the birds and deceitfully reassure them that it's safe to land. The successful hunter is concealed in wait for the ducks arrival, often for hours, often while wet and cold.

Everyone I know who hunts waterfowl does so with a 12-gauge shotgun, usually a pump, sometimes a semiauto or an over–under double. I can't remember the last time I saw a side-by-side double in a duck blind, but I'll bet there are still a bunch of fellows out there using them.

UPLAND GAME

There is little in the shooting sports more enjoyable than taking to the fields on a fine, crisp autumn day in pursuit of pheasant or quail. However, I consider the pursuit of upland game to be more of a shooting activity than actual hunting. In many countries, the activity is in fact referred to as shooting, rather than hunting, and the participant is a shooter or a gun, rather than a hunter. True, birds must be located, but that's mostly left up to the dogs or in some places, the beaters.

In England, for example, a line of beaters drive up the birds from hedgerows and underbrush while the shooters take the birds as they come. Shooters usually proceed in a sort of skirmish line or wait in line with each man's field of fire invisibly marked out by agreement, so as not to shoot one's fellow shooter. It is not unusual in England for a gun to bring down thirty birds in an afternoon's shooting. Each bird must be paid for. I'm told that today's going rate is sixty pounds a bird. At the current exchange rate, that amounts to one hundred dollars for each pheasant.

The approach in the United States is roughly the same, although somewhat more democratic in terms of cost, and we don't use beaters. We do progress across fields in lines with fields of fire agreed upon or understood between shooters. Sometimes, in the heat of the moment, mistakes are made. In combat, such mistakes are called friendly fire. Such accidents in upland shooting are not considered particularly friendly.

HUNTING ADVICE

My main advice for hunters is pretty straight-forward.

- Use enough gun, but no more than you can handle.
- Shoot within the limits of your gun and your skill.
- Do your homework, and know the habits of your quarry.
- If you're going to hunt, master the skills to become a *hunter*—not just a shooter.

CHOOSING A HUNTING GUN

Generally speaking, whatever arms your state allows you to legally hunt with will do the job—if the hunter does his. This is not to say you can't take pleasure in a fine firearm. When you select your hunting gun, pick one that calls to you. If you have a gun that you really like, you'll practice more and shoot better with it.

Another suggestion is to arrange to try out a friend's guns or go to a rental range where you can try various guns before making your decision. You'll quickly determine if you're recoil sensitive. Almost everyone is. Those who say they are not have, for the most part, trained themselves to ignore recoil. If you're at all recoil sensitive, choose the lightest legal caliber and practice extensively with it before taking to the field. If you're one of the few who are unaffected by recoil, choose whichever caliber you like, but make sure you get a good deal of practice with it before going after game.

BOLT-ACTION RIFLES

There is little mystery left in bolt-action rifles. Mauser got the rotating bolt sorted out more than a hundred years ago. And the bolt gun, in general, is well understood by all its makers. There are only two bolt guns that I have any personal feeling for. One is the Springfield 1903 in its original chambering, .30-06. After I had shot a friend's 1903 extensively, I bought one, though my funds were extremely limited. I disliked the stock and restocked it with one having less drop and providing a straighter line of sight, which was more suitable for my particular cheek-to-stock weld. It did everything I asked of it.

The .30-06 has fallen from favor due to the advent of the .308. This is understandable, given that the .308 is our service cartridge, has a shorter case length, and thus is chambered in shorter actions. You can do most things with a .308 that you can do with a .30-06, but there are still more loadings available for the .30-06. As has been proven time and again, with the proper loading, you can take anything from squirrel, maybe a little overkill there, to brown bear. I won't tell you the .30-06 is better; I just like it.

My all-time favorite bolt-action was a Mannlicher Schönauer with the graceful and slender full stock, short carbine-length barrel, and butter-knife bolt handle. Chambering was in the classic 6.5x54mm cartridge. The rifle balanced like no other—quick to the shoulder and easy in the hand. The action was as silky smooth as a lover's skin. The smoothness of the action was due to fine machining and polishing. To my eye, it was simply a sweetheart—a beautiful little rifle that would take anything from mountain goat to elephant if the shooter did his part.

I bought it in the old Abercrombie & Fitch. No, not the store that sells pre-worn-out jeans and t-shirts at absurd prices to suburban teenagers. The old Abercrombie & Fitch stocked virtually every worthwhile firearm on the planet plus clothing, luggage, and gun cases like you can't imagine unless you've been to a hunting store in Paris. Teddy Roosevelt shopped there, as did every outdoorsman of note, and quite a few of us who were not at all notable but happened to have a couple extra bucks. I don't remember what I paid for the Mannlicher. All that mattered was that I had enough cash for the little rifle, five hundred rounds of 6.4x54mm, and a saddle leather case that made my Louis Vuitton carryall look like a reject from a garage sale.

Part of my infatuation with the Mannlicher was the sheer romance of the rifle and caliber. W. D. M. "Karamojo" Bell used it. Hemmingway used it. It had to be right if Papa shot with it. Aside from all the romance, the rifle and caliber combination really did work. The little 6.5x54mm chambering in the hands of Bell and others took thousands of African elephants and Cape buffalo, two of the most dangerous and hard to kill animals on our planet. This was due to the high sectional density of the projectiles; they were long and heavy in relation to their diameter and capable of deep penetration through muscle and bone. This combined with low recoil made for easy, accurate shot placement into vital organs, such as the heart and the brain—Bell's preferred target. In his books,

Bell writes of taking more than a thousand elephants, mostly with brain shots, some of them while they were charging.

How did one of the world's greatest hunters achieve his success? He did so by having intimate knowledge of the game and habitat and by choosing a weapon that was accurate, comfortable to shoot, and up to the job. Shot placement, not power, was the key to his shooting.

You can pick a gun with your head. You can analyze power and trajectory; so much of this and so much of that and you'll probably get a good gun. But if you ever find a rifle that calls out to you like that Mannlicher did to me, grab it and hold onto it like a drowning sailor clutching a lifesaver, because you'll have found *your* gun.

MODERN HUNTING RIFLES AND SHOTGUNS

Remington, Winchester, Marlin, Savage—all American rifle and shotgun manufacturers, and they make terrific products. So do the European makers. I've never seen a bad Browning, Beretta, CZ, Sako, or Steyr. You can't go wrong with any of them. The standard of manufacturing quality in terms of fit and finish vary, but in terms of function, any of these will do. I doubt if there's a bad rifle or shotgun made in America or Europe these days.

BOLT-ACTION RIFLES

- **Browning** has a great line of centerfire rifles, all of them nicely finished.

- **CZ's** rifles are uniformly of high quality. They make a handy little full-stock carbine that balances well, and they have a full range of large calibers.
- **Dakota** rifles are considered state of the art today. Most of their offerings cost about the same as a good used car.
- **Kimber** makes a few models, all priced in the low four figures with the same quality as their pistols.
- The **Remington** 700 Series is probably the most popular centerfire rifle being made in America today. It does pretty much everything right and is available at a price that is affordable for the middle range of hunters. (See image on page 68.)
- **Ruger** rifles, like their handguns, are famous for durability and good performance. They are available in dozens of variations and all popular calibers, all at reasonable prices. (One of their older models, the International Carbine, is close in concept, if not in actual design, to the old Mannlicher.)
- **Sakos** are made in Sweden to a high standard. The Swedes know a good bit about making quality rifles. They are currently imported to the United States by Beretta.
- **Savage** is an old and well-regarded name in American arms. They make a wide range of good, affordable centerfire rifles.
- **Steyr** is still making excellent rifles in a variety of models at good prices considering their quality. The Steyr Mannlicher Classic SBS (Safe Bolt System) bears a resemblance to their old carbine and is available in a twenty-inch barrel, as well as twenty-three- and twenty-six-inch barrels. My old Mannlicher had an eighteen-inch barrel.
- **Weatherby** continues as a premium American-made rifle with a model that will suit anyone who can afford them.

LEVER-ACTION RIFLES

I was never bitten by the cowboy bug, so I never developed an affection for lever rifles. But many love their lever guns and do excellent work with them. The lever-action .30-30s made by Marlin and Winchester have probably been used to take more deer in America than any other rifle. Fast on follow-up shots and handy in its carbine lengths, it is an American icon.

- The **Winchester** is now discontinued, but **Marlin** keeps the lever-action flag flying and makes an excellent, accurate rifle in a wide range of models.

Marlin Model 336C lever-action .30-30 Winchester. © Marlin

- **Browning** also has a lever-action in the game. The Browning lever gun has a detachable box magazine with the Browning traditional exceptional fit and finish.

Feeding a round into the magazine of a Winchester .30-30.

Winchester .30-30 rifle with tubular magazine.

Browning BLR Lightweight Stainless.
© Browning

PUMP RIFLES

- **Remington** makes pump, or slide-action, rifles in calibers from .22 to .308. This is a good choice for the shotgunner who wants to maintain a similar action in both rifle and shotgun. I had one in .30-06 and liked it.

Remington Model 572 BDL Fieldmaster, which shoots .22 S, L, and LR. © Remington

Remington Model 7600 Synthetic. © Remington

SEMIAUTOMATIC RIFLES

Most centerfire rifles have a military appearance, with notable exceptions being offered by Benelli, Browning, Winchester, Remington, and Ruger's handy little Mini-14 series. There's nothing particularly wrong with going afield with a military rifle as long as the magazine is blocked so the number of rounds on tap conform to your local fish and game regulations. You may get some odd looks from fellow hunters, but most military rifles are accurate enough for hunting and far more durable than a sporting rifle.

Ruger Mini-14. © Ruger

For those who prefer an autoloader, you will find the Benelli R1, Browning BAR, Remington Woodsmaster, and Winchester Super X to be perfectly suitable for large game. Ruger's Mini-14 series is chambered for .233, which many states confine to small game. The Ruger is also chambered in 7.62x39mm, which is legal for deer in most states.

Browning BAR Safari. © Browning

Winchester Super X Rifle. © Winchester

MILITARY SURPLUS RIFLES

Military surplus rifles are generally either bolt guns or semiauto. Many are quite reasonably priced and serviceable.

Surplus Mauser bolt-action rifle (top); Mosin–Nagant bolt-action with Scout Scope (bottom).

MOSIN–NAGANT

I have recently seen this rifle at ranges around the country. Many hunters use it with good results. Lyudmila Pavlichenko, a famous Russian female sniper, scored more than three hundred kills against Nazi armies with this model rifle.

Even more impressive was Simo Häyhä and his use of the Mosin–Nagant. He was a Finnish sniper in the Winter War in 1940 when Russia invaded Finland with more than 160,000 men. Against incredible odds, a few thousand Finns held off the Russian Army and extracted a terrible toll. Simo Häyhä became known as the White Death due to his killing more than five hundred Russian soldiers, many of them at farther than four hundred meters with iron sights.

The rifle was designed in the late nineteenth century and was used by various armies well into the twentieth century. It is still highly functional today. Not as finely finished as a commercial-grade sporting rifle, it is inexpensive and has the robust build of a military firearm. It obviously has good accuracy.

SCOPES FOR YOUR HUNTING GUNS

Most hunters today, whether after elk or bunny, scope their rifles. There are distinct advantages. You can see your target better from a longer range. It can be easier to get and hold a good sight picture, as you don't have to line up a front and rear sight. Your sighting is all on one visual plane. Today's rifle scopes are generally quite sturdy and not subject to the fragility so many scopes suffered from in years past, though they are not as sturdy as iron sights. Scopes can be divided into two general types: variable and fixed.

Variable Scopes

The 2x4 power scope is a popular selection for all-around deer hunting in woods or forested mountains. Two by four means that the image is magnified from two to four times. For open prairie, many shooters go to a 4x12, which obviously makes the image much larger. Some might think that bigger is better, but not in this case. Bigger is just bigger. When magnification is increased, the field of view is narrowed. If, for example, you tried to use a 12X in the woods, you wouldn't be able to see the forest for the trees or the game for the leaves. Varmint and target shooters will go up to 18x32. This works for them since magnification is more important to them than field of view.

Thompson/Center Contender single-shot rifle with variable scope (top); Ruger No. 1 single-shot rifle with variable scope (bottom).

Thompson Contender with variable scope.

Fixed-Power Scopes

About the only shooters who use scopes and don't use variables are handgun hunters and riflemen who adhere to the scout rifle idea. Most handgun hunters seem to go with a fixed 2X scope, as do the scout rifle shooters. The scout rifle concept includes a low power scope with long eye relief mounted well forward. There are various reticles—you might think of them as the crosshairs, except there are many more options in aiming points than crosshairs.

Surplus Mauser with variable scope (top); Mosin–Nagant with Scout fixed scope (bottom).

Leopold and Bushnell are two well-known makers of good quality and reasonably priced rifle scopes and other optics. Zeiss produces optics of the highest quality. There are at least a dozen makers of good scopes, but a review of them all is beyond the limits of this publication.

Bushnell Elite 2.5–10x50. © Bushnell

In spite of the advantages, I rarely hunt with a scoped rifle. It may be true that today's game is more wary than in the past, and it's harder to get close enough to shoot without a scope. But for me, it's as much a matter of style as anything else.

I'm not starving. I can choose my method. I don't mind using my lungs and legs, getting down on my belly and crawling, or spending two days slowly working my way close enough to a mulie's bed to take a shot from close range. I like the feel of the earth, the sound the leaves make in the wind, and the scent of a deer at ten yards. I started hunting this way when I was a kid, and a rifle scope was so far beyond my reach I never considered owning one; thus, I often hunt without one.

COMMONLY USED RIFLE CALIBERS FOR HUNTING

.223

Some states allow the hunting of deer with the .223, but most do not. Most states confine its use to varmints and small game.

A Native American acquaintance, Sam, took me shooting in New Mexico. Sam, after coyote skins, had his Marlin .22, so he "wouldn't ruin the pelts." I was along for the ride. At first light, just about the time when you can see your front sight, Sam started calling. I was to his left side. His rifle was ready at his right shoulder. He used his left hand to call. If I hadn't been next to him, I would have sworn that some poor bunny was in his death throes. The first coyote came in from my side at a dead run and skidded to a stop about thirty feet in front of our position in the brush. Sam dropped him with one shot to the head. Sam took four coyotes from that stand, one of them a quartering shot at fifty yards with the animal at a dead run away from our position. At about eight o'clock he called it a day.

.243

This is, in most places, the entry level for deer hunting—adequate power, flat shooting, and easy on the ears and shoulder.

.270

A necked down .30-06, the .270 shoots with a flatter trajectory than any of the .30-06 leadings. Some consider this a good elk cartridge, while others think it's too light for the big guys.

.30-30

The .30-30 in a lever-action carbine is the all-American deer cartridge and gun. Easy to handle and shoot with good terminal ballistics, this one will work as well today as it has for decades.

.308

The .308 is our former service round (NATO 7.62) and is still in use in various specialized roles. It is a good choice for an all-around big game cartridge. The same caliber as the .30-06, it is essentially a shorter case version of that round.

.30-06

The "06" was first developed in that year, 1906. It was used in the Springfield, the M1 Garand,

and a hundred different sporting rifles. It is still an excellent all-around cartridge.

.300 Winchester Magnum

This is an accurate round with a flat trajectory commonly used for long-range and large-game hunting. It is popular for elk and kicks like a Missouri mule. Remington makes some ammunition they call Managed Recoil that recoils less but with some loss in performance.

There is an entire range of rifle cartridges more powerful than those I have listed. However, in my view, none of them are a good choice for a beginning shooter.

HANDGUNS FOR HUNTING

Many people, even veteran shooters, regard handgun hunting as a stunt or something beyond the reach of any normal shooter. It is not. Handguns are perfectly good tools with which to harvest game. The only caveat is that they must, like all weapons, be used within their effective range, limits of power, and according to the abilities of the individual shooter.

Smith & Wesson Model 29 .44 Magnum.
© Smith & Wesson

Elmer Keith, a famous shooter and author who lived from 1899 to 1984, wrote that he made a six-hundred-yard killing shot on an elk with a Smith & Wesson four-inch barreled .44 Magnum. Some folks do not believe Elmer made that shot. I do. But that does not mean I could make that shot or that you could.

However, I do believe that if you can't hit a small paper plate every time at fifty yards with your weapon of choice, you have no business being afield. That's a pretty minimal level of marksmanship, but it will get you game if you can get close to your quarry. Any decent handgun will meet that standard and many will far exceed it. I have an ancient Walther .22 that will reliably hit beer cans at seventy-five yards. I had a 9mm HK P7 that would bang steel plates at a hundred yards every time. Like Elmer, I have an S&W four-inch .44 Magnum that makes me look good when I shoot it. The unschooled think I'm [insert hero's name here] when I blow up tomato juice cans balanced on the range markers at one hundred yards. But I'm not. Lots of people can shoot guns like these as well as or better than I, some much better.

Walther .22.

If the notion of handgun hunting intrigues you, give it a try. After you've established a minimum level of marksmanship with that .22 target pistol, of course. That same .22 is also the best pistol to make your hunting bones with. Start with squirrels and rabbits, and see where it goes. It might go all the way to a big pistol and big game. States have regulations governing the taking of game with pistols, as they do with all other weapons. Check the regulations before taking to the field.

COMMONLY USED HANDGUN CALIBERS FOR HUNTING

.22 Rimfire

As you now know, the .22 is every beginner's caliber and every expert's caliber. The automatics I recommend in chapter 1, "A Case for the .22," are a good place to start.

Beretta U22 Neos. © Beretta

Browning Buckmark 22. © Browning

S&W M22A. © Smith & Wesson

.357 Magnum

How times change. The .357 Magnum was once touted as The World's Most Powerful Handgun. Advertising copy said you could take everything that walked, crawled, or flew with it. Today it's considered barely adequate for rabbits. A four-inch Smith & Wesson Model 19 in .357 Magnum was my first centerfire hunting handgun. I took my first elk with it. I don't think today's wild critters are any tougher than they used to be. If you like the .357, it'll do the job. Smith & Wesson, Ruger, and a bunch of others make good revolvers for this caliber.

Smith & Wesson Model 19.

Ruger single-action .357 prepared to fire.

10mm

The 10mm is the only common auto pistol round that's legal to use to hunt large game, and that's only in some states. As of this writing, there are only a few pistols chambered for it, with the Colt Delta Elite and the Glock 20 and 29 coming to mind. The Glock 29 is the lightest weight of that small group and more accurate than you might think. Banging steel plates rapid fire at fifty yards is no trick at all. I carry the little Glock as a trail gun in areas where creatures roam that are sharp of tooth and claw.

Glock 20/20C 10mm. © Glock

Glock 29 10mm. © Glock

.44 Magnum

Smith & Wesson, Ruger, and others make excellent .44 Magnum revolvers. The four-inch Smith is my personal favorite. Almost twice as powerful as the .357, it kicks like a short-changed customer at an enlisted man's beer bar. But I don't mind it—probably because I don't try to fight the recoil. I just ride with it. No way can I shoot it as fast as, say, the Glock 10mm. Maybe someone can, but not me. I only use it for hunting not self-defense.

I have hunted bear and wild boar with a handgun, both of which are somewhat dangerous. Both can be taken with a bow using the right methods. Nevertheless, you might want a more powerful weapon than what you use for deer. Brother Bear can get angry with someone who puts a bullet in his bottom. Better make that first shot a good one.

Ruger Redhawk .44 Magnum.

HUNTING SHOTGUNS

A FEW GUNS AND LOADS FOR WATERFOWL AND UPLAND GAME

Many of my friends and I shoot Remington 870s in 12-gauge—a shotgun that has served legions of hunters for many years and still does so today. The venerable 870 is probably the most popular shotgun in America. Winchester also makes an excellent pump shotgun, as does Mossberg. All the aforementioned companies also make semiautomatic shotguns. With today's ammunition, the autos are equal to pump guns in reliability. We mostly use number four shot, but conditions vary and you might want to go to number two.

I have known men who would no more pursue upland game with a pump gun than they would serve rotgut moonshine to their guests in place of single malt scotch whiskey. In truth, a pump-action Remington, Winchester, or Mossberg will bring home just as many birds as the finest Beretta or Browning double in the right hands. Just because the birds are put up by dogs doesn't mean you don't have to be a good shot to get them.

The over-under doubles used by many upland game shooters are not cheap. The least expensive doubles from Beretta, Browning, or Benelli will set you back a couple thousand dollars, and the more expensive models are two to three times as much. Brands such as Perazzi are in the if-you-have-to-ask-you-can't-afford-it range.

PUMP-ACTION AND SEMIAUTO SHOTGUNS

Virtually all shotgun makers build both pumps and semiautomatics that can be used for waterfowl. Today's semiautomatics are as reliable as the pump actions. Benelli, Browning, Mossberg, Remington, Savage, and Winchester all make good guns in a range of finishes.

A few traditionalists use doubles for waterfowl. I would encourage you to do so if you are attracted to the graceful lines and incomparable handling of the double. (If you would like an in-depth look at shotguns, rifles, or handguns, I recommend that you buy the *Shooter's Bible*, which is an exhaustive listing of firearms with prices and specifications.)

THE TAO OF THE HUNT

With the exception of upland game or waterfowl, when I go in search of game, I go alone. In fact I often also go after upland birds alone. True, I've many times been hunting with groups, but I consider those to be social events, not serious hunting. I may travel to a hunting area with friends, but when we reach our grounds, I go alone.

I also practice the Tao of the Hunt. As I wrote in chapter 7, Taoist techniques have nothing to do with religion and everything to do with directed attention. These are methods used by native peoples in many parts of the world that were codified centuries ago. What follows is a thumbnail description of this process.

ENTERING

First, go to your chosen hunting grounds. Of course you have selected a location where there actually is game or at least the possibility of game. There is no point in attempting to hunt elk in the Florida Keys or wild boar above the tree line. You must know your quarry, its habitat, and its habits. You can gain most of this knowledge from your local library or experienced friends. But as one of my teachers once told me, wisdom is the combination of knowledge, experience, and reflection. In other words, do your homework, then pay attention to everything around you in the wild and learn to gain experience.

When you reach your chosen hunting grounds, let the patterns of thought you have used to get there slip away as you walk from your vehicle. Forget about the highway and the traffic. Forget about work. Leave all that behind and let the familiar constrictions of your mind slip away as you move into the natural world.

Find a spot that *feels* right to you and stop. Sit or stand as long as you're comfortable. I generally find it best to sit or even lie down when doing an entry. I often choose a place just inside a tree line where I can see without being seen.

You've already done your homework. You don't have to endlessly review details regarding your quarry's habits. Thoughts will bubble up. Let them drift away. Direct your attention to the immediate environment. See what there is to see: pinecones, rabbit droppings, a blue jay's feather. Don't analyze these details; just note them.

Close your eyes and extend your awareness as far as you can, through woods, across meadows, and up the mountainside. Wherever you happen to be, extend your awareness and awaken all your senses: feel the wind moving, smell the cold granite, the musty leaves, or the tannin from the dark swampy stream behind you; hear the skittering of dry leaves, the breathing of the fox that's watching you, the drip of early morning dew from the limbs above you. Sink into and become part of everything around you.

SEEING, CALLING, STALKING

Now visualize your quarry—deer, rabbit, boar, or bird. See the creature as if it were standing in front of you. Retain awareness of your surroundings, but focus on *seeing* your quarry in your mind's eye. Then ask your quarry to come to you or tell you where it is.

Yeah, yeah, I know. It sounds like new age crystal stuff, but it works—sometimes. Nothing works all the time, but this will greatly improve your hunting success if you put it into practice.

When you have become part of the field, swamp forest, or mountains, and when you have *seen* your quarry, move to a place where you will await your quarry, or begin the slow stalk to your quarry.

Continue to watch and see and feel everything around you, above you, and under you. If you've decided to select a stand, make sure you've blended into the bushes, rocks, or whatever your immediate environment is. Don't move. You might think you're not moving, but if you haven't practiced the art of stillness, you are probably moving something. A deer can spot the flicker of an eyelid at fifty yards. Blink slowly. Visualize your quarry coming into your field of view. Wait. Be still. Be ready. Wait.

If you are stalking, move with the forest. Blend your movements with the wind and leaves. Move slowly. No that's too fast. Move even more slowly. Move upwind. Forget about time. My watch goes in my pocket when I'm stalking game. Time is determined by the movement of light and breezes that rise in the morning and drift down in evening. Let your mind be calm. Look carefully at every detail in your surroundings as you move slowly and quietly. You're not on a sidewalk; don't city walk. Walk so you're in balance, so you could freeze in any position, on one foot or two. Do not slam down your heels. Touch your foot down softly, and roll from heel to toe. Feel the wind, if there is any, on your face and drift slowly and quietly to and though the area where you think your game will be or you have sensed that it is.

When I moved over the crest of the hill and down to those mulies in their bed, I was moving so slowly that if I had been crossing a room it would have taken me about a half-hour to get from one side to the other, maybe longer. But I didn't know how long it was taking. It could have been an hour or a week. My mind was clear with no hunter's energy, no thoughts of the shot I might take, no plan to do anything other than what the moment brought to me. I was a ghost, a cloud, a drift of leaves—part of the forest. Also, I was wearing moccasins and an old soft wool shirt, both of which helped me to blend and move quietly.

When I sat with my back against an aspen waiting for my first elk, I had brought a folded space blanket to sit on. But the cold came up through it. At first I was cold, but after a while, cold wasn't cold. At first my nose itched. Then it didn't. Or, if it did, I didn't mind it. I sank back into the tree and became the tree. I sank my roots deep into the ground and stretched my limbs wide and watched the days and nights pass.

Of course, I didn't really sit there for weeks and become part of the tree. Nor was I doing drugs. I used age-old methods that have been well understood and codified by monks and shamans, used by hunters and warriors, and passed down over generations. I imagined becoming the tree. I visualized it. In doing so, I subsumed my consciousness into the tree and stopped radiating hunter's energy. In effect, I created a cloak of invisibility. After some time, I wasn't there. There was only the mountain and the tree. That's why the elk passed me by.

There's much more to the Tao of the Hunt: walking silently and balanced, being unseen, seeing, hearing, smelling, and perceiving. You can read about these things and more in my book *The Tao of Survival*.

CHAPTER 9

Care and Cleaning for Your Gun

I actually like the smell of Hoppe's No. 9. I guess that makes me a gun nerd or a gunny; on second thought, there's no guessing to it. Hoppe's No. 9 solvent and bore cleaner has a distinctive scent. Anyone who's been shooting more than a couple of decades is familiar with the smell. It has been as much a part of my shooting as the smell of cordite. That's because cleaning the guns was a ritual I carried out after each shooting session. Not much has changed.

There are a number of new cleaning solutions, and some of today's firearms—Glocks, for example—have finishes that will withstand a lack of care better than the traditional blued steel. But you should always clean your guns after you shoot them. It's the right thing to do. Besides, you don't want a failure to fire due to a gummed up firing pin just when you squeeze off a round at that moose you went all the way to Alaska to find, do you?

The famous Hoppe's No. 9. © Hoppe's

The old way was to first unload your gun and put the ammo away. Then field strip the firearm and slather Hoppe's No. 9 over all the metal parts and scrub the bore with a brass brush dipped in the solvent. Then you got a toothbrush and dipped it in the solvent and scrubbed every steel surface you could find. After that, you let everything sit for a while to give the solvent time to dissolve all powder residue. Then you ran patches down the bore until they came out clean and wiped down everything to remove the solvent and powder residue. Finally, you lightly oiled all the steel parts and reassembled the piece.

You can still do it exactly like that today, and it will work just fine. You could also use one of the modern cleaners, such as those shown on this page. They all work. Some of them are one-step cleaners. Using the one-steps will make the cleaning process somewhat easier, but you won't get to smell Hoppe's No. 9.

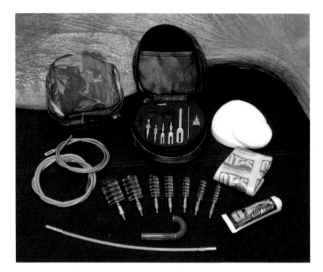

Otis Hard Core Hunter Cleaning System. © Otis Technology, Inc.

through the wire, or Brother Bear decided he was really angry and wasn't going to let you shoot him again. The two most common causes for failures leading to catastrophe are:

1. Failing to clean the gun, resulting in gummed up and inoperative working parts.
2. Over oiling. Too much oil can cause as many problems as not cleaning at all.

This is particularly so in tropical and desert environments. In dry, sandy areas, grit and sand blow in the wind and get into everything. Grit and sand will stick to oil and gum up the mechanism, causing it to fail to function. In wet tropical areas, everything is attracted to oil, including many bugs. The best thing is to run slightly dry. A thin film of oil is what you want.

Too much lubricant, especially some of the highly penetrative substances, can also seep into your ammunition and render it useless. Keep your ammo dry. It does not need to be lubricated.

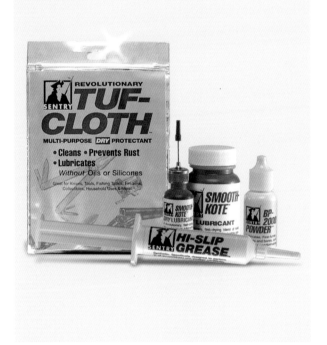

A Sentry cleaning kit. © Sentry Solutions Ltd.

Okay, all kidding aside. Keeping your gun clean is serious business. More than one person has lost his or her life due to a dirty gun. The problem is not that the gun blows up, although that could happen. The more likely problems are a failure to fire or jam at a critical moment, say when a platoon of bad guys was coming

Two important points:

1. Always, always, always—I repeated it three times so you would get the idea that this is important—UNLOAD YOUR GUN AND PUT THE AMMO AWAY BEFORE YOU START TO CLEAN YOUR GUN. I used all those capitals for the same reason. We've all heard the stories about the guy who shot himself while cleaning his gun. Don't be that guy or girl.

2. Clean your gun. If you want the gunnies to respect you, keep your gun clean. Rust loves steel, and all gunnies hate rust worse than a preacher hates sin on Sunday morning. A filthy, rusted gun is a disgrace to its owner and an insult to its maker and to civilization itself. There's no need to promote entropy, it doesn't need any help.

Part III:
Gun Safety

CHAPTER 10

Personal Responsibility

Gun safety begins with the acceptance of personal responsibility for your firearm and ammunition. I'll repeat that. Gun safety begins with the acceptance of personal responsibility for your firearm and ammunition. This is the most important statement that can be made on the topic of gun safety. Read it, understand it, let it soak into your bones, and live by it. It may one day save your life or the life of another.

My grandfather gave me my first rifle, a Remington single-shot .22, which was a popular choice in those days for a first gun due to its inherent safety. A single-shot has no magazine, and it is a simple matter to see if the chamber has a round in it. My grandfather told me that responsibility accompanied privileges, and that I would always be held accountable for my rifle.

I remember his words after he handed me my rifle, "You now possess an instrument that gives you the power to take life. Take heed and behave in a responsible manner. Never take any life by accident—not the life of any human, friend or enemy, and not the life of any creature. Take no life by accident and by intention only for food or if your life is threatened." (My grandfather was born in 1863 and really did talk that way.)

He also instructed me in the following simple rules:

- **Always** know whether your rifle is loaded or not. Loaded or not, always handle it as if it were loaded.
- **Always** know where your rifle is pointing.
- **Never** point your rife at anything you are not prepared to shoot.
- **Never** place your finger on the trigger until you are ready to fire.
- **Never** fire until you are sure of your target.

- **You are responsible** for your rifle at all times, whether or not it is in your immediate possession.
- **Never** allow your rifle to be handled by anyone of whom you are not sure.
- When your rifle and ammunition are not in your immediate possession, **you must lock them** in your trunk.

In more than fifty years of shooting, I have never yet found anything wrong with those instructions. There was more. He showed me how to safely handle my rifle so the muzzle was always pointed toward the ground or a place where there was no danger of hitting anyone. He also taught me marksmanship. When hunting, he said I must shoot to kill cleanly so as not to cause unnecessary suffering and that I should not take the shot unless I was sure of a solid hit.

Although we live in a different world now, some things do not change. When you purchase your first firearm, you must accept personal responsibility for your firearm and ammunition. Aside from the morality of the matter, the law requires it. You must have control of your firearm and ammunition at all times. If they are not in your immediate possession, they must be secured. You must also acquire the knowledge you need to handle and use your firearm responsibly, safely, and effectively.

READ YOUR MANUAL

Although we will cover basics, a responsible gun owner will read the manual that comes with a new firearm, learn how the safety devices on his or her particular firearm operate, and use them appropriately. If the firearm did not come with a manual, one should be obtained by contacting the manufacturer. In the case of older guns, manufacturers may no longer have manuals or be out of business. Manuals for virtually all firearms can be located, often by contacting various online resources.

GENERALLY ACCEPTED SAFETY RULES

Here are three simple safety rules endorsed by the National Rifle Association and responsible shooters. There is some overlap between the NRA rules, those practiced by generations of responsible gun owners, and Gun Safety Rules According to Ayres.

1. Always keep the gun pointed in a safe direction.
2. Always keep your finger off the trigger until ready to shoot.
3. Always keep the gun unloaded until ready to use.

The NRA has eight or nine additional rules, most of which are similar to Gun Safety Rules According to Ayres. Many organizations and local governments have formulated their version of gun safety rules. I advise you to read all the NRA rules and others you come across and consider them carefully. Safety is the first and highest priority of every responsible shooter.

SAFETY IN GUN HANDLING

STEP ONE

Develop gun awareness, which means knowing where your firearms are at all times. At first this may seem burdensome. In fact, it is no more so than knowing where your car is located. Use whatever memory devices you are familiar with, but make sure to always know the location of your guns and ammunition.

STEP TWO

Develop muzzle awareness, which means knowing where your muzzle is pointing at all times. At first muzzle, awareness requires constant attention. After a while, it is no more difficult that being aware of the moving and shifting traffic around you when driving.

Once you have those two things firmly in memory, safe gun handling becomes straightforward. Here are a number of safe and unsafe handling practices.

DO safely pass a firearm with the muzzle pointed at ground.

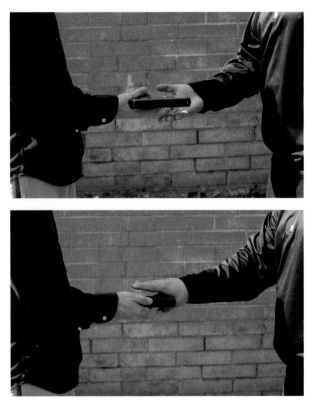

DON'T point the muzzle at a bystander.

DON'T pass a firearm in an unsafe way.

Slide closed, muzzle pointing at wall—SAFER.

Muzzle pointing at ground—SAFEST.

CLEARING YOUR GUN

Clearing means to unload the gun by removing the ammunition and opening the chamber so it can be seen to be empty. The magazine of a semi-auto should be removed, even if there is no ammunition in it. All guns should be cleared and open before being passed from one person to another. However, on occasion a person might hand you a firearm with the bolt or slide closed. This might happen in a sporting goods store where clerks might be untrained or in any other situation where an untrained person is handling a gun. If this happens, clear the gun as soon as you have it in hand.

When someone hands you a gun, you automatically clear it, even if you saw that person clear it—and the other way around. This may sound redundant, but it's a sound practice.

A fellow once handed me his new custom .45 to admire with the muzzle pointing at me. He had removed the magazine but had failed to retract the slide. I stepped to one side, slowly and carefully grasped his gun-holding hand, and pointed the muzzle to the floor. "What's the matter?" he asked. "It's empty." He released the pistol to my hand. While still pointing it toward the floor, I retracted the slide and a bright, shiny .45 cartridge flipped out of the chamber and fell to the floor. The fellow's mouth dropped open and his face went pale. "I thought . . ." he stammered.

"Uh-huh," I said.

Anyone can make a mistake. Assume personal responsibility and be a safe gun handler. **ALWAYS CLEAR ALL GUNS.**

Extracting a fired round from a Ruger single-action revolver .44 Magnum.

Extracting fired cases from a Smith & Wesson Model 19 double-action revolver.

Ruger .44 Mag. single-action with the loading gate open.

There are a number of accompanying photos illustrating proper and improper ways to clear a gun.

DO pass a firearm with the bolt open.

Pistol cleared, slide open—SAFE.

DON'T check the chamber with the muzzle pointing at a person.

SAFE—checking the chamber with the muzzle pointed at the ground.

SAFE—passing a handgun, chamber open.

SAFE—releasing the slide, muzzle toward ground.

SAFETY WHILE SHOOTING

EYES AND EARS

Always use protection for your eyes and ears while shooting. Many older shooters, myself included, have suffered some hearing loss due to inadequate or no hearing protection. Ear protection devices look like either plastic earmuffs that go over your ears or foam inserts that go inside your ears. Both types work well. Eye protection consists of glasses with impact resistant lenses. You can purchase good quality eyes and ears from any gun shop. Make sure they fit comfortably and securely. Most ranges will provide eyes and ears to those who do not have them. From what my sons tell me (as best I can hear them), you can lose a good bit of hearing at concerts, also. So, maybe ear protection is second nature for some young people.

Shooting glasses protect your eyes from the possibility of a ruptured cartridge, which is rare, or the more common back splatter and general debris.

Proper ear protection.

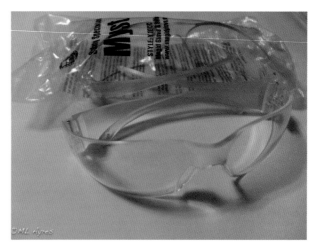

Proper safety eyewear.

SAFETY AT THE RANGE

Read and obey all range rules wherever you happen to be shooting. Aside from being safer yourself, you will be respected by experienced shooters. All of us watch each other when we first meet to determine others' gun handling habits. No knowledgeable shooter relaxes around shooters he or she doesn't know until he or she sees how they handle firearms. Bad safety practices will earn you a friendly, or not so friendly, warning. Continued unsafe behavior might result in being requested to case your gun and attend a safety class.

Range rules vary a little from place to place, but not much at cold ranges, where all guns are unloaded unless they are on the firing line and guns are pointed only downrange in the direction of the targets. Eye and ear protection is to be worn at all times. While this may seem like common sense, it is important to always stop and read the ranges rules before entering a range. Also, as in golf, tennis, and other sports, common courtesy is always appropriate and welcome.

TYPICAL RANGE RULES

- All firearms must be unloaded and cased when brought to the range. Revolvers without cases will be carried by the top strap with the cylinder open. Semiautos will have the slide locked to the rear, or open, with the magazine out. Long guns, when uncased, must have the action open and muzzle pointed up.

- Firearms may be loaded on the range only when pointed downrange, at the firing line, and at the assigned stall.
- Only authorized firearms and ammunition may be used.
- Use of eye and ear protection is required at all times.
- While on the range, firearms must be pointed downrange at all times.
- If a misfire or other malfunction occurs, keep the firearm pointed downrange and signal the rangemaster.
- Do not fire at unauthorized targets or shoot across lanes.
- Do not move forward of the firing line. If anything falls forward of the firing line, contact the rangemaster for assistance.
- The use of alcohol or drugs is prohibited on the range. Persons under the influence of alcohol or drugs are prohibited.
- Smoking, eating, or drinking is prohibited.

At hot ranges, guns are always loaded. This is typical at combat matches, and a somewhat different level of awareness is required. Rules at hot ranges vary somewhat, so in the interest of avoiding confusion no typical rules are given. Odds are, you'll visit your first hot range in the company of someone who will guide you. If you're on your own, read the posted rules and ask someone to help you get oriented. The shooting fraternity is mostly made up of friendly folks who are pleased to help you get into shooting.

Some people simply will not follow common safety rules. There is no place for that person on a shooting range or in a hunting field with others. It's rare to see unsafe behavior with experienced shooters, but it happens.

I was once at a range where a local instructor was working with a student who was obviously new to shooting. The student walked downrange to inspect his targets with his 1911 .45 in hand. This was a cold range. I noticed his slide was forward, the hammer cocked, and the thumb safety down.

I politely pointed this out to the trainer. He told me to mind my own business. I thought my safety was very much my business. I spoke to the rangemaster about the safety violation. The rangemaster and the instructor were pals, and he also felt it was okay for an unschooled shooter to be walking around with a loaded, cocked, and unlocked auto. Considering that this student had already covered the entire firing line with his muzzle, I disagreed. I cased my gun and left at once, meanwhile keeping a close eye on the student. I would advise you to do the same in a similar situation. Ultimately, you are responsible for your own safety.

SAFETY IN THE FIELD

Muzzle awareness, awareness of your companions, knowing where your bullet or shot will go before you pull the trigger, keeping good fields of fire, moving correctly with a firearm—all these things are fundamentals of safe gun handling in the field. Specific detail about safety in the field can be found in chapter 8 on hunting. However-, stay alert and follow the basic rules, and you should be good to go.

DRINKING AND SHOOTING

Don't do it. If you feel like getting liquored up and howling at the moon, lock up the guns first. Alcohol and gunpowder is an explosive mixture—not one you want to fool with. If you would like a celebratory bottle of Bollinger after bagging that moose you've chased all over Montana, a nice glass of Chateau Lynch-Bages with that duck you just shot, or a couple bottles of Budweiser after Bowser flushed those quail and you bagged them, case the guns first. No exceptions. Let me repeat that: **Unload and case the guns before pulling that cork or opening that bottle.**

Local Customs

I once went hunting on a jungle-covered island in the Southern Philippines with a bunch of Filipino guys who loved to get red-eyed on *tubâ*, a particularly foul concoction made from, I think, palm sap. We spent hours thrashing through the underbrush, well into the night. These guys were rowdy and getting pretty thirsty. But when we finally got back to their village, even these guys knew to unload the guns and put them away before hitting the tubâ. If they had not done so, I would have done it for them. Local standards vary, but none require me, or you, to be put at risk.

WHERE BULLETS GO

You've probably wondered where all those bullet holes in road signs on country roads come from. They come from criminally irresponsible people who have guns, cars, and booze but no common sense or regard for others. Those bullets that make holes in road signs continue on until they hit a tree, cow, or possum minding its own business, or they go through a window and into someone's home, where folks are probably sleeping soundly and not thinking about a bullet that might come slamming through a wall and into their baby's crib. But I know none of you are the kind of people who would do that. No, not my readers. No way.

Every Fourth of July and New Year's Eve, some irresponsible people fire their guns into the air, and others are injured or killed by those projectiles. Do not fire your gun into the air. The bullet (or shotgun pellet) that goes up eventually comes down, sometimes on someone's head. Contrary to urban myth, bullets do not disintegrate in the sky. They always come down somewhere. Always.

HOW ACCIDENTS HAPPEN

"It went off."

No, it did not. Guns do not go off by themselves. Guns are relatively simple mechanical devices and have no life or volition of their own.

If your gun fired and you didn't mean for it to do so, you made a mistake. Accepting personal responsibility for your guns is both the first and last thing you must do. Accidents happen when a gun owner fails to accept his or her responsibility.

In conclusion, imagine this scene: a platoon of recruits shivering in a grey dawn. An icy wind knifing through their thin clothing; a light snow rests on the frozen ground. A platoon sergeant who looks like he has fought in every war since the First Peloponnesian passes along the rows of new soldiers and hands them each a rifle, along with some words of instruction.

When it was my turn, he took a rifle from the stack carried by the corporal assisting him and handed me an M1 Garand rifle. I accepted it, held it at port arms, and slammed the bolt back to inspect the chamber and ensure it was empty. I then stood at inspection arms. He put his face close to mine, about an inch away, and said while looking deep into my eyes, "This is YOUR rifle. YOU are responsible for it. Drunk or sober, shot up, blown up, wounded or sick, blind, crippled, or crazy, YOU are responsible for this rifle."

He didn't scream or bug out his eyes like a movie drill instructor. He spoke seriously with gravity and great intensity of purpose. Then he paused for a moment, assessing me, and asked quite gently, "You got that soldier?"

"Yes sergeant," I said. "I got it."

And I did get it. I hope you get it, too.

CHAPTER 11

Trigger Guards, Gun Cases, and Other Safety Devices

TRIGGER GUARD

Invented centuries ago, the trigger guard protects the trigger from being struck or pulled accidentally. Virtually all firearms have them, with the exception of certain small single-action revolvers, such as those made by North American Firearms. When using a gun with a trigger guard, you must put your finger inside the trigger guard to reach the trigger.

Do not put your finger inside the trigger guard until you are ready to fire. Instead, anchor your trigger finger on the receiver just above the trigger guard. The trigger guard is a simple piece of metal that has doubtless prevented many accidents and will prevent many more.

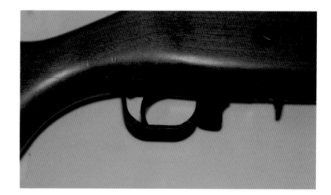

Trigger guard.

GUN SAFETIES

Although safety devices are particular to individual firearms, in general they work by blocking the trigger of the firing pin. Accompanying photos show various types of safeties on a variety of different guns to give you an idea of what to look for. Remember, you must study your owner's manual and practice with your unloaded firearms until the operation of your safety is second nature.

There is little hope for anyone who, having been properly instructed, chooses not to use safety devices and handles his or her firearm in an unsafe manner. Such persons should take a good look at themselves and their motivations. If they are not willing to accept the responsibility that comes with firearms, they should acknowledge this, accept their own limitations, and not own guns.

Shotgun safety OFF.

FN Five-seveN safety OFF.

Remington 870 pump-action shotgun safety OFF.

Shotgun safety ON.

Remington 870 pump-action shotgun safety ON.

GUN CASES—SOFT, HARD, LOCKABLE

Inexpensive good quality cases, both hard and soft, are available in every local gun shop. Many jurisdictions now require hard cases for transportation of firearms. Check your local laws. Virtually all jurisdictions require guns to be in a case, hard or soft, and locked when being transported. The exception to this requirement is if you have a concealed carry permit, which is discussed in part IV on self-defense.

When traveling with guns, I make it a practice to lock each gun into its individual case. I then put those cases into my locked car trunk or into another locked bag or case if traveling by air. At home, a responsible shooter will unload all firearms not in use and lock them in individual cases. Locking those cases in a safe or another locked container provides another level of protection. Ammunition is always locked in a separate container. This means that an unauthorized person wanting to load a firearm would have to first locate the firearms, locate the ammunition, get through three locks, and figure out how to load the weapon. Something as simple, and yet so important, as locking cases and separating ammunition could change the outcome of a situation.

Plano shotgun case. © Plano

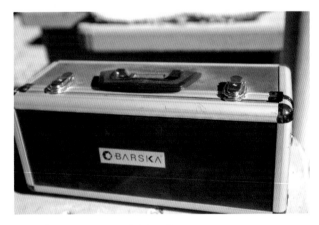

Barska gun case. © Barska

Plano pistol case model 10089. © Plano

Plano soft rifle case. © Plano

GUN SAFES

Formerly gun safes were expensive propositions and only the dedicated shooter would own enough valuable firearms to justify the purchase of a safe. This is not so today. Dozens of reasonably priced safes in a variety of sizes are readily available. If they are not in stock at your local gun shop, the proprietor can order one for you. Some guns safes have a quick-open feature, which can be a good thing for that one gun you might wish to keep loaded and accessible in case of need.

Fort Knox safes. © A.G. English

Gun Vault safe. © Gun Vault

TRIGGER LOCKS

In recent years, we have been deluged with requirements for the gun owner to obtain and use trigger locks. Now it seems that the gunmakers are required to include them with each firearm. This may or may not be a good thing. I suspect that anyone who is responsible enough to actually engage a trigger lock will already use a locked case or safe.

Trigger guards, safeties on firearms, gun safes, cases, and trigger locks are only tools and are useless if not properly employed. Accepting personal responsibility is the first and most important step toward becoming a safe and responsible gun owner who is not a hazard to his or her fellow citizens.

CHAPTER 12

Kids and Guns

I grew up around guns. I never saw or heard of an accident involving guns in my family. In addition to the hunting rifles and shotguns we had at home, my grandfather carried an S&W Bankers' Special in a slip holster in his pocket. Each day when he got ready for bed he took his revolver from his pocket, in its holster, and put it on the nightstand next to his bed.

When I was about four or five I asked my grandfather if I could see his pistol. He took it from his pocket, unloaded it (explaining to me that he was doing so), and handed it to me. He explained the parts of a revolver. He also told me why he carried it, and that I was never to touch his pistol, all in terms I could understand at that age. He promised that when I was old enough he would show me how to and let me fire it. Which he did. My grandfather treated me with respect and taught me about responsibility and honesty. I would no more have touched his revolver than I would set my dog, Brownie, on fire.

My sons have all grown up around guns. None of them have ever once, even as children,

done anything stupid or unsafe with a gun. Or had any accidents. I credit this to proper education and a firm and clear understanding of a gun's potential. As my grandfather taught me, I taught my sons.

When my sons first developed curiosity about guns, my wife and I began a dialogue with each of them. We explained that guns, like cars, were for adults, and that when they were older, and if they wanted, we would teach them how to shoot as we would teach them how to drive a car.

If they asked to see my handgun, I would unload it and let them examine it. There was nothing to hide or be secretive about. Then I would put it away and reinforce previous explanations: guns were for adults; they were not for kids, because kids could get hurt.

Guns were private family business not to be discussed with friends. Above all they were not to ever try and locate any of the family firearms, to play with them, or to allow friends to do so. Later, when they were old enough to understand,

I demonstrated to each of my sons the potential power of a gun. In addition, all guns in our home were always under lock and key, except for my personal handgun that was always under my immediate control.

At a very early age, different for each one, they were instructed in simple rules:

- A gun cannot hurt you by itself.
- You can hurt another person with a gun.
- Another person can hurt you with a gun.
- Therefore, do not touch any gun you might see.
- The family guns were not to be touched or discussed with any friends.
- If you see a gun, go directly to an adult and tell them.
- If a friend wants to play with a gun, do not do so. Leave at once and get an adult.

When the boys were old enough to understand consequences and accept responsibility, *and when they said they were ready AND I thought they were ready*, I taught them gun handling and marksmanship, one step at a time. My youngest had little interest in guns until he was fourteen. My oldest and middle sons were ready at ten. When they were ready for their first rifles, I taught them what my grandfather had taught me about safety and responsibility, all of which is at the beginning of chapter 10.

In addition, I had one rule that could not be compromised, a tough one for ten-year-olds, not so much for a fourteen-year-old. Before they could have their first rifle, they had to give up all of their toy guns and make a commitment to never again play with toy guns. No exceptions. I drew a clear and unwavering line. To add weight to the moment, I also had them read and copy down the following:

"When I was a child, I spake as a child, I understood as a child, I thought as a child; but when I became a man, I put away childish things."

Tough stuff for kids. But not as tough as a foolish accident and a dead kid.

BOY SCOUTS

When I was ten or eleven, I joined in the Boy Scout marksmanship program. On Friday I would take my rifle to school with me. This was well understood and accepted by school authorities. After school I pedaled to the local city park that had a small-bore range where the Boy Scout program was held. My sons look at me in disbelief when I tell them things like this about my childhood. Understandable, given the nature of today's world.

I recently met a man who is doing his part to give some kids a lot of fun while teaching them valuable skills and responsibility. Brian Dillon runs the Southern California Boy Scout marksmanship program. When Brian told me about his activities, I said that I thought that whole thing had been blown away with the sixties. It was. But Brian brought it back to this one place. Basically, Brian *is* the Southern California Boy Scout marksmanship program, along with a bunch of kids.

If you have kids and you want them to learn how to shoot and to learn the core responsibility that should be attached to guns, contact

Boy Scout Troop 104 at a troop-to-troop competitive shoot, scoutmaster Brian Dillon bottom left. © Brian Dillon

Members of Troop 104 cleaning rifles—a merit badge qualification requirement. © Brian Dillon

Boy Scout Troop 104 at the firing line. © Brian Dillon

your local Boy Scouts. If they don't have such a program, ask them to revive the old Boy Scout marksmanship program. If the Boy Scouts aren't interested, there is always the National Rifle Association's youth programs. My youngest son honed his rifle skills with the NRA and so have thousands of other kids.

The National Shooting Sports Foundation suggests these safety rules for kids:

1. Don't go looking for firearms, in your house or a friend's house. Don't let other kids look for firearms in your house.
2. If you find a firearm in your house—or anywhere else—leave it alone. Don't touch it! Don't let anyone else touch it! Tell an adult.
3. Even if a firearm looks like a toy—don't touch it! Some real firearms look like toys. Don't take a chance. Tell an adult.

In general these rules sound pretty good. My only concern is with the third sentence of rule 2, as that could lead to a struggle between children. I would prefer a child to walk away.

The most important thing is a dialogue. When kids and parents are talking openly and freely and when kids have clear boundaries and understand that boundaries are not arbitrary but for their own good, it's less likely that they will get into trouble.

Kids and guns? Sure, they go together just fine.

Part IV:
Self-Defense with Firearms

CHAPTER 13

An Approach to Self-Defense

The subject of armed self-defense is one of utmost seriousness—and one that is too often treated lightly. Doing violence to another person in the real world has nothing in common with ballet-like choreographed movie violence. Violence is an ugly thing. It is a thing that will remain in your memory if you have the misfortune to witness or take part in such an event.

I will discuss this subject based on my experience and observations and will do so in a realistic manner. Therefore, some of the language that follows will be, of necessity, a little rough, in some cases graphic, but no more so than needed to make certain points. It is not my intention to shock, and I do not pander to those who enjoy vicarious bloody war stories. I recount certain events to only instruct and do so only in consideration of the possibility that such instruction might save the lives of good people.

When Native Americans first encountered Europeans with guns, they concluded, based

on their observations, that the Europeans' guns produced a loud noise that killed by shock. Many people today have beliefs about firearms that are equally erroneous. Few peaceful civilians in our culture have witnessed someone being shot. Fewer still have taken part in a gunfight. Most people get their impressions from movies and television. Based on these fictional depictions, many seem to think that a handgun functions as some sort of paralytic device. The actor pulls a trigger, the movie gun makes a loud noise, and someone falls down, often with no evidence of injury, or perhaps a small smear of fake blood. In more graphic films there may be a lot of movie blood. There may even be some special effects and acting that simulates real-world wounding.

We all know that movies and television are fiction. We may even know that the movie gun is a prop incapable of firing live ammunition, and the noise is added in when the sound track is completed. But repetitious viewing creates the unconscious belief that this is how guns work in the real world. They do not. This belief is as incorrect as the one held by first contact Native Americans. Guns are basically highly sophisticated rock throwers. They are not instant paralytic rays.

REALISTIC CONSEQUENCES

When a person fires a handgun at another person, he or she usually misses. If he or she does hit another human target, the bullet makes a hole in the person. This usually results in a great deal of pain and much blood, more than you might imagine if you haven't witnessed such an event. When someone is wounded, he or she often thrashes around, screams, curses, cries, runs away, or perhaps falls down, depending on a universe of variables. Various body tissues are sometimes exposed or ripped from the body. An expression, which seems to be popular these days in movies about criminals, is brains on the wall. This is not just a metaphor. When a powerful bullet breaches the cranial vault, brains do get splattered on walls, and elsewhere, along with bits of bone and other body tissues.

It is far more traumatic to witness this sort of thing in real life than to watch a sanitized, choreographed movie. If you have had such an experience, the odds are you will experience a post-traumatic psychological effect, whether you are the person who pulled the trigger, the one who got shot, or a bystander. If you are the agent of such violence, you will find that the only way to live after having done this to a fellow human is if you were totally justified in your actions. If you have fired a gun to save your life or the life of a loved one, or to prevent rape or other violence, you will have the consolation of knowing you acted righteously. But you'll still carry the weight and the memory.

As a moral person trying to defend yourself, you do not shoot with the intention to kill. But it is impossible to shoot with the certainty that you will only wound. No matter how much skill you have, once the bullet leaves the muzzle, it can bring death to another. Your intention should be simply to stop the assailant, but things happen fast in violent encounters and there are no guarantees. Moreover, it is virtually impossible to cause such a stop without risking a lethal result.

I often hear rough and casual talk about shooting and killing. This talk usually comes from people who have no experience of being shot at, shooting at another person, or in fact, of any violence other than the schoolyard variety. Such talk grates on my sensibilities, as it should on yours. Soldiers objectify their enemies to function and do what their duty requires of them. Rough, dehumanizing talk is sometimes part of a soldier's life. It should be no part of being an armed civilian.

Five hundred years ago, John Donne wrote, "No man is an island, / Entire of itself," also pointing out that "Any man's death diminishes me." This comes down to us as literature, and like much great literature, it contains a simple truth. If you have the great misfortune to be placed in a situation where you must take another's life to survive, the experience will change you, and not in any movie macho way. It will diminish you.

We live in a random and sometimes violent world. Any of us might be forced to use violence to protect a loved one or ourselves. The only thing worse than being forced to do violence is to witness the death or violation of a loved one or to have such done to oneself. The decision to arm or not to arm yourself is yours alone. It is not mine.

I am neither an advocate nor an opponent of armed self-defense. Arming oneself is a moral issue with legal consequences—an issue that each must decide for himself or herself. If you have made your decision, and if the decision is to arm yourself, the following information may be of some value to you.

> ### Legality of Defense
> I am not a lawyer. I offer no legal counsel. You are responsible for your own actions. Learn the laws that govern violence and self-defense and abide by them.

ALTERNATIVE MEANS OF DEFENSE

There are means of self-defense other than firearms. Pepper spray, impact weapons (such as sticks, canes, and heavy flashlights), and edged weapons all come to mind when one is threatened. No matter what weapon you use, a less than lethal defense is always desirable.

Over the years, I have traveled in dangerous places and encountered threatening circumstances when, due to my immediate situation, I was not armed with a firearm. Yet, like many others in tight spots, I found a way to prevail. Sometimes thinking outside the box is enough. Other times, it is not.

If faced with an armed assailant or a group of assailants, a gun may be your best tool, since the gun is a more effective weapon than anything else readily available. However, if your only tool is a hammer, you tend to see all problems as nails. Try to have an alternative to the gun in place. Personally, I eagerly await the invention of the temporary paralysis ray.

In the first volume of his much beloved trilogy, *The Lord of the Rings*, J.R.R. Tolkien's character Frodo tells Gandalf the wizard that Gollum deserves to die for his deeds. Gandalf counsels Frodo, agreeing with him that Gollum does deserve that, but telling him, "Do not be too eager to deal out death in judgment." *The Fellowship of the Ring* is a fantasy book, but Gandalf's statement is wisdom.

THE USE OF THE GUN FOR SELF-DEFENSE

Many people immediately think of a gun, most often a handgun, when they think of defending themselves from criminal assailants. This is understandable. There are good reasons why Samuel Colt's invention—the first reliable, easily portable, repeating handgun—was called an equalizer. A good handgun combined with sufficient skill can enable a small, physically weak person to defend his or her life against larger and multiple assailants. Sufficient skill is the key point. Mere possession of a firearm will not make you a world-class gunfighter any more than buying a saxophone would allow you to play like Chet Baker.

You must learn to use your firearm as a self-defense tool in order for it to be an effective self-defense tool. This should be self-evident, but based on my experience and observations, it is not. Ranges today are packed with people banging away with a variety of handguns and wrinkling their brows in confusion when they fail to hit their targets. Yet, as their conversation indicates, these same folks leave the range convinced their new 9mm or .45 will protect them. It will not.

Guns are inanimate objects. They are not talismans or amulets with magic powers to protect you from evildoers. The gun will not protect you from anything. You must assume the obligation of protection or assign it to another. I also hear these new gun owners talking about how they will shoot better when "they" are coming at them. Probably not. Odds are that they will not rise to the occasion, but will fall back in frozen panic or worse, spray rounds everywhere—perhaps hitting bystanders.

During the 1992 Rodney King Riots in Los Angeles, I was besieged by emotional requests from a few non-gun-owning close friends for the loan of a firearm. Outside of my family, only close friends, fellow professionals, or sporting friends have ever known that I possessed firearms or had any expertise with them (in my adult life). When I was a kid, everyone had guns. Today's climate is different. Also, many years of professional discretion have created certain habits. I received similar emotional requests from two friends in Washington, DC, during the riots of 1968 that followed the assassination of Dr. Martin Luther King, Jr. On both occasions I refused to provide firearms to my friends. Why? Was my refusal coldhearted and callused? No, it was not.

In a Central American capitol city, during a civil disturbance in which hundreds were killed during the first night, I received a similar request from an associate with whom I had spent the evening the violence broke out. We were holed up in the bar of an international hotel. I gave him my backup pistol without question. Why would I arm this friend but not the others?

I did so because my friend in Central America knew how to defend himself with a firearm. He was not a danger to himself or to the innocent. The friends who asked for guns in Los Angles and Washington, DC, did not know how to shoot, had no knowledge of basic gun handling, and had never fired or owned guns. Being able to actually use one in personal defense was a skill as remote to them as playing that saxophone like Chet Baker. I was not willing to arm untrained people who might shoot innocents, themselves, or me by mistake. It would have been irresponsible to do so.

It would be equally irresponsible for you to arm yourself and go forth thinking you are prepared to defend you and yours before you have acquired a minimum level of competence. Although it is preferable to get capable instruction, many have taught themselves to shoot well. Others have learned the basics from books and then practiced until competent.

But what about those friends I left unarmed? Were they left to the mercies of the mob? Certainly not. I did not, and would not, leave my friends to fend for themselves. I offered to personally defend any and all who wanted to move into my home for the duration of the disturbance and any who were in my company while out and about. I also offered to provide basic armed defensive training when time permitted.

No one is immune to error, professionals included. We can all miss our mark and send a lethal round screaming down a city street. But we can avoid the obvious pitfalls of arming inexperienced, untrained, and frightened people.

SERVICE HANDGUNS

STOPPING POWER

Most experts in this field advise the novice to choose the most powerful handgun that he or she can control, the minimum being one of the service calibers. The argument is that you need all the stopping power you can get, and less powerful cartridges, sometimes scornfully called subcalibers or mouse guns, are inadequate for self-defense in that they have marginal stopping power. This point of view has merit but ignores certain realities having to do with the definitions of control and stopping power. It also ignores other realities regarding daily carry for civilians. Service calibers tend to come in handguns that are either too large or too heavy for daily civilian carry in a low threat zone, which most of the United States is.

The argument about what constitutes stopping power is one that has a long history, continues today with more heat than light, and will likely rage on until the invention of that paralytic ray. Among experts, there is much disagreement. Entire books are devoted to this ongoing discussion. For our purposes, let's stipulate that modern service calibers are up to the job required of them (if the shooter does his or her part), but that none of them are the hammer of Thor.

More powerful calibers cause more shock and create larger wounds than less powerful calibers. This means shots that strike an assailant, but not in a vital place, *might* have a better chance of stopping the assailant. But that's not written in stone. Many factors come into play in an armed encounter, one of which is psychological rather than physical. Some will faint when shot in the arm with a .25. Others will continue to fight when shot in the chest with a battle rifle round, such as a .308. However, many studies by government agencies, including various military units, have established that 85 to 95 percent of the effectiveness of any shot is determined by shot placement, not power.

Service calibers are, for the most part, capable of penetrating auto bodies, doors, and walls, a desirable feature for armed professionals who must be prepared to engage in full-on firefights. Service calibers are also more effective at extended distances. However, few civilians can justify shooting through walls to hit an assailant, and most civilian armed encounters take place at close distances, often arm's length. Therefore, I do not think that a service caliber is always the best choice for self-defense by the average civilian, especially one who is not a gun enthusiast or otherwise willing to devote the time and effort required for mastery of the service weapon.

DIFFICULTY OF USE

Service handguns have considerable recoil and are difficult to shoot accurately without training and practice. Few civilian novices who are not planning to go into a profession requiring professional-level shooting are going to obtain the training or do the practice required to master a service handgun. Notice I said master—not control. Mastering a handgun means acquiring the ability to hit your mark under field conditions, which might mean in darkness, on a slippery icy street, when you're sick and scared and your hands are sweaty and your heart is pounding and you're breathing fast, and while you're trying to protect your child who is screaming and crying. You must do so every time and fast. Simply being able to keep your rounds on a silhouette target at close range on a sunny day at the local shooting range isn't a high enough level of skill to allow you to claim mastery.

Of course, a .45 ACP, a .357 Magnum, a 10mm, a .40, or a 9mm will deliver more power on target than, say, a .32. The question is, will it do so in your hands, in rapid fire, in poor lighting, when you're under extreme stress and everything is moving fast? If you can't claim this level of expertise, you might be better served with a less powerful caliber—one that you can master with the amount of training and practice you can and will devote to the pursuit.

Oh, by the way, they're called handguns, not *handsguns,* for a good reason. Two-handed fire, such as we now see in movies and the news, is all very well when possible. Many trainers only teach two-handed shooting. Shooting with both hands is more accurate and is preferred at longer ranges. But what about when you're using your off arm to hold your child behind your back while returning fire? How about if one arm has been injured? What if your assailant is only three feet away from you and closing fast or already on you?

One fellow I know has been to a school of combat handgunnery where he was taught to always shoot with two hands. With a firm two-handed grip he can, more or less, control his .45. That is, he can get most of his shots on a silhouette target, most of the time. When he shoots one-handed the muzzle flips up—way up—and it takes him a long time to get back on target. In one-handed rapid fire, he's lucky if his shots go downrange. Yet he's convinced he can control his .45. He might be able to better control a less powerful handgun, but he is also convinced that it is the .45 he must use—nothing else will stop a bad guy. This sort of mindset simply will not do. If you want to defend yourself with a handgun, learn to shoot your handgun of choice with one hand, as well as two, and learn to use it under all conditions you might encounter.

THE FLINCH

Although I discussed the flinch in a previous section of this book, I will discuss it here as it pertains to armed self-defense. The most common cause for misses that I have observed is the anticipation of recoil and muzzle blast leading to jerking the trigger—or pushing, pulling, or heeling the gun—which moves the handgun out of alignment. This is commonly called a flinch. I've had occasion to shoot with many armed professionals, including uniformed police officers, undercover agents, covert operators, and active duty armed servicepeople. Some of them have had flinches the size of Mount Rushmore. I'm sorry if that disillusions you, but most armed professionals are just regular folks who work at acquiring their skills.

There are few geniuses of the gun, such as Bill Jordan or Jelly Bryce, and even they practiced a great deal—more than most nonprofessional civilians ever will. I have no knowledge whether either of those great shooters ever developed a flinch. But take a look at Bill Jordan shooting a .44 Magnum in his excellent book *No Second Place Winner*. In one very clear photo, Bill Jordan demonstrates the folly of choosing a weapon more powerful than you can master. Although his service weapon was a .357 Magnum and he was a consummate master of it, he wrote that a pocket-sized, alloy-framed revolver loaded with .22 Magnums was a good hideout gun and superior to the same revolver chambered for the .38 Special. Jordan thought that the .22 Magnum was a highly effective round, faster in rapid fire than the .38, and the saving in weight over a .38 was a significant matter for everyday carry. These assertions come from one of the finest shooters of all time—a man who was a master of highly powerful weapons and survived many armed encounters.

A flinch is no disgrace. As I previously wrote in chapter 3, I've had one. Like the measles, I got over it. The cure is more training. With proper training and practice, a dedicated person can overcome a flinch. But it takes time and work—more time and work than many nonprofessionals are willing to commit to the process.

The basic technique of diagnosing a flinch is to have a coach load a dummy round in your magazine without telling you which is the dummy round. When you squeeze the trigger on the dummy round, it will become immediately apparent if you have a flinch. The diagnosis is also part of the cure, which I detail in the "Foundations of Marksmanship" chapter. However, some people simply cannot get over a flinch induced by a powerful gun. For them, a less powerful gun is a better choice than a gun they cannot control.

Every time I go to a public range, I see people banging away with two or three different 9mm, .40, or .45 pistols that someone told them to buy, usually on the grounds that these were what they needed to stop an assailant. These folks are always shooting at silhouettes, and they are usually missing them. At best, they get a few rounds somewhere on the silhouettes at a range of about seven yards. They're thrilled if they manage to get a cluster of shots the size of a basketball anywhere on the target. The concept of a group doesn't seem to exist for them. They switch from handgun to handgun, presumably thinking that one or another will provide the magic required for them to consistently hit the target. All of them—not some, all—are flinching like Mel Gibson's character in *Lethal Weapon*.

Will this sort of shooting serve to save them and their loved ones in a lethal encounter? Maybe. If they fire enough rounds at their assailant, they might get lucky—again forgetting about whom else might get hit with those stray rounds. On the other hand, maybe not.

Remember, 85 to 95 percent of the effectiveness of any shot is determined by shot placement. Under stress, you will be more likely to hit your target with a gun you are comfortable with rather than with one that you are not. Hitting a vital spot is the most important part of the entire process, not the caliber. If you can hit a small paper plate at twelve feet while drawing and shooting fast ten out of ten times with a .32 and two out of ten times with a .45, with which gun do you think you're better armed?

CONCEALABILITY, PORTABILITY, AND CARRYABILITY

If you obtain a concealed carry permit, which you must apply for with your local police, you will learn that one of your obligations as a legally armed citizen is to keep your weapon concealed from public view. The larger the gun, the more difficult this is to accomplish. Most service handguns are for many people, especially the small-framed and women, too large and heavy to carry totally concealed all day.

That may not apply to you. You may find no problem with daily carry of a service handgun. However, the odds are that unless you are in a high threat environment or an armed professional, you will eventually leave your service weapon at home. Why? Because service weapons are not especially comfortable to carry. Most police officers I know are relieved to get home and take off their guns at the end of their duty shift. Not one uniformed police officer I know carries his service weapon off duty. They choose something smaller and lighter. Do you think a civilian shooter will behave differently? Odds are that big gun will stay home.

I once read a comment that a highly regarded trainer, a shooter of the first order, supposedly made in reference to carrying a service handgun, "It's supposed to be comforting, not comfortable," or something like that. That's a clever zinger. But it does not change the reality that even with a good holster, you're still toting a couple pounds of steel on one side of your body—not the best prescription for avoiding the orthopedist and chiropractor. And it isn't comfortable, even with a good holster. It's a price professionals must pay. Is it one you are willing to pay?

PROFESSIONAL TRAINING

Professional instruction can be a significant shortcut to the acquisition of armed defensive skills. The National Rifle Association can refer you to a local instructor who has been certified to teach basic skills, which is where a new shooter should start. This basic instruction will give you a foundation, but it won't make you a gunfighter.

There are schools available to private citizens where they can obtain training from highly qualified professionals. But there are also obstacles to attending a shooting school, including cost. Most schools appear to offer a fair price, considering the attention given and the potential skills that can be acquired. However, it's a price that many cannot afford. In addition to the cost in money, there is the cost in time. I've heard the argument that anyone who is serious about armed self-protection should make the time and find the money to get proper professional training. The reality is that few of us have excess time or trust funds. Most will not or cannot manage to attend a shooting school.

Besides, there isn't room for everyone. Based on the number of training facilities in the country, the average class size, and the number of classes that are offered each year, it would appear that fewer than 1 percent of those who buy handguns for self-defense would be able to take such a course, even if it were free.

There are eight million new gun owners in the United States each year. About half of them are buying guns for self-defense. The US Army couldn't train four million people each year. Throw in the Marines, and we still couldn't do it. This is far more people than all of our armed services and civilian training schools combined could train each year. Further, based on the available numbers, most people who buy handguns for self-defense don't even join a local gun club or get basic NRA instruction.

What do the remaining 99 percent do—the ones who get no formal training? They might buy books such as this one and others written on the topic, hopefully the ones recommended here. They get some instruction from a friend, family member, or someone they meet at a range. They practice a little, maybe a box of ammo or

two, and call it a day. Is this enough to enable a person to defend themselves with any handgun, let alone a .45 or a 9mm, both of which clearly require more work to master than, say, a target .22? Maybe. Maybe not. The universe is a chancy place. They might get lucky.

Note that I said defend themselves. I'm not discussing combat hand gunnery, tactical hand gunnery, or any variation of these activities, which are the topics upon which many of the shooting schools are focused. Self-defense is an entirely different matter than clearing a building filled with hostages and terrorists. By self-defense, I mean engaging at close range one or more hostiles who have the intent to do you or yours mortal harm, at close range. According to available statistics, the distance between body contact and twenty feet takes in the great majority of assaults on persons.

To expect the average citizen to reach a level of expertise with a service pistol only achieved by highly trained professionals, and to task him or her to do so without the weeks of training and the thousands of service-caliber rounds professionals expend, is to set him or her up for failure. Many of those who do minimally qualify with the skills taught at some schools don't continue to practice, and their skills degrade over time.

There is also the matter of personal inclination. The first handgun I ever formally trained on was the Government Model 1911 .45 ACP. I loved it. I shot "distinguished expert" (an army qualification level) with it after a few days of training and practice. But there were others—healthy, strong, young men who might have been headed for combat—who did not qualify with the .45. Why? The training was certainly adequate. I think the answer is simple. Some people, even soldiers, just aren't into guns. They don't particularly like them. They have no talent for the gun and won't put in the work required for competence. And make no mistake, it takes work to become accustomed to the muzzle blast and recoil of a service pistol, to master trigger control, and the other skills that go into defensive marksmanship.

What then do we say to these folks? "Oh well, if you can't handle the right gun, too bad for you. There's always pepper spray and prayer. Go forth and hope for the best." No, I don't think so. There's an alternative for them: less powerful handguns. Handguns that are easy to shoot well. It is important to master the kind of effective defensive training that stays with you and doesn't require weekly visits to the shooting range to retain.

SHOT PLACEMENT

As I stated earlier, studies carried out by various government organizations clearly demonstrate that between 85 and 95 percent of the effectiveness of any shot is determined by shot placement. Understanding this is of the highest possible importance. Not caliber, not stopping power, but bullet placement is the most important determinant of effectiveness.

Bullets work by striking the central nervous system or the blood circulation system and interrupting the flow of blood or neural impulses. Shocking power is a factor in the more powerful cartridges. But how much shock it takes to put down a particular assailant and how much is delivered by a given cartridge is subject to much debate and varies a great deal from person to person. The pain of a small caliber wound in an extremity might stop one person, while multiple center-of-mass hits from the most powerful service calibers might, and have, failed to stop others.

What we know is this: if neural impulses stop, the person stops. Quickly. If the blood supply is stopped, the assailant also stops, but more slowly. Again, the details of all this are beyond the scope of this book. For our purposes, let's take it as a given that a less powerful round placed in a vital spot is more effective than a powerful round in a less effective location or a miss. And a miss is what most untrained people shooting a service weapon under highly stressful defensive conditions will achieve. Many trained people, including police officers, do the same under real-world conditions.

No number of powerful misses will stop an assailant as well as one well-placed round of moderate or low power. And let's not forget that those misses are going somewhere—maybe into an innocent bystander. Aside from the moral implications of wild fire and stray rounds, there are also legal liabilities. Remember, you are responsible for every round you fire.

I see that many experts now consider an area about the size of two legal pads in the center of a silhouette to be the critical zone; they say if you can hit this zone on a nonmoving target, there is no need to be any more accurate. Further, we are told that you must use your sights and both hands to achieve this level of accuracy at seven yards. If you can hit this area most of the time in daylight while standing still and shooting with both hands while getting a good sight picture, you're supposedly competent in defensive shooting. I don't think so.

When I was learning to shoot to live, our instructor pinned playing cards to the silhouettes, face out, and told us to focus on the pips. We started with single shots at two yards using one hand. The idea was to focus on a small part of the target, thereby better ensuring that we would get a good hit on a vital spot, or if we missed, we would miss by a small margin. After we could hit the playing cards with regularity, we took a giant step to the rear and started over and so on until we found the distance at which we needed to use our sights.

We were told that in combat we should focus on, say, a button or an eye, rather than the whole person. This is similar to advice given hunters to not shoot at the whole animal. The point of all this was to make us understand that the only way to stop an assailant for sure was to hit a vital point. We were training to do exactly that.

If you train to shoot small groups on a silhouette rather than shooting at the whole silhouette, when you are faced with an actual threat, the odds are better that you'll hit your mark. Those small groups will open up under stress. If you've been shooting, say, three-inch groups, they'll probably open up to six inches but will still be on target. If you've only trained to shoot center of mass with groups or patterns the size of a legal pad, those groups will open up too, likely leading to missing the target altogether.

Low-light shooting with so little light you couldn't see your sights and shooting in full darkness was another activity—one that occupied about a third of our training. At night, you cannot see the pips on a playing card and maybe not the card or even your sights. Our focus then was to shift to the center of mass of our target, which was all we could see, and to fire bursts—two or three rounds fired rapidly. But here, too, the training to shoot tight groups paid off with more hits. We also trained on moving targets and moving targets at night, and again the practice of shooting small groups at close range while focused on the target rather than the sights proved effective.

FIGHT, FLIGHT, FREEZE, OR FLAP

All of us have heard of the flight or fight syndrome, the response coded into our species at the level of DNA. We perceive a threat, our bodies shift into fight or flight mode, and we do one or the other. That's what we're told. There are two other responses I have observed that are equally common. I think the fight or flight syndrome could be more accurately called the fight, flight, freeze, or flap syndrome. This topic, and fear control, are subjects that should be studied by anyone who is serious about armed self-defense and survival. I go into these topics in depth in my book, *The Tao of Survival*.

Briefly, people don't only flee or fight. They freeze. This is also known as the deer in the headlights effect. It often happens to people who don't have a clue as to how to deal with a situation or even any frame of reference for it. It also happens to people who get stuck in many different choices and can't decide which action to take before it's too late. My training sergeant used to say, "Don't just stand there. Do something, even if it's wrong." The idea is to get out of the way of an oncoming train, even if you have to jump into a ditch and maybe twist your ankle.

People also flap. This is a term I first heard from a British SAS trooper. To flap means to move fast and frantically doing irrelevant things that won't help the situation, kind of like a hog on ice—lots of squealing, legs and hooves every which way, but no forward motion.

Too many choices, complicated training methods, too little practice to get reactions into reflex, or no training at all lead to freezing or flapping, and that can be deadly.

FIGHT LIKE YOU TRAIN

I've often heard the statement, "You'll fight like you train." Maybe, maybe not. If your training has been too complicated, if you haven't had time to absorb it, and if you haven't continued the practice required to retain the skills, there is an excellent chance you'll forget everything and freeze or flap. Unless you have spent a few weeks training as a full-time job with excellent professional coaches, you're probably not going to be able to run that M4 carbine at the same level as a Special Forces operator running and gunning in Afghanistan. And it's unlikely that a weekend seminar in combat handgunnery will serve your needs if armed assailants attack you.

What's the answer? How can you acquire life-saving skills without joining the military or spending a fortune at private training schools, many of which will still not provide you with the simple, effective, durable training you need?

DEFENSIVE SHOOTING

If you want to become a well-rounded marksman, go to the "How to Shoot" chapters in part II and learn the fundamentals first. Also, as suggested there, contact your local NRA instructor for some hands-on training. If you are only concerned about self-defense and looking for the maximum return on investment, go with the combat masters: Fairbairn & Sykes, Applegate, and Jordan. Reference the following books to find the methods I was trained in: *Shooting To Live* by Captain W.E. Fairbairn and Captain E.A. Sykes, *Kill or Get Killed* by Colonel Rex Applegate, and *No Second Place Winner* by William H. Jordan. I do not have the level of experience that these men had, but I have used these methods and adapted them. In life-threatening situations, they have proven effective for me, as they have for thousands of others.

The skills these men, and I, advocate are relatively easy to learn and easy to retain. There are some variations in method from one to the other, but basically we're all singing in the same choir. My personal methods are drawn from these sources and adapted to my needs and experience, which includes years of training in martial arts and leads to my use of a mobile and stable shooting stance drawn from martial arts.

Once learned, a relatively modest amount of practice—about one thousand fully-focused live fire rounds—will get them coded to reflex. Another thousand rounds of dry fire will help to embed those reflexes so that they become part of you.

A key point in this training is that these methods follow natural reflexes that humans revert to when threatened. Therefore, if the new reflexes you develop follow the ones you have as original equipment, you are less likely to freeze, flap, or have your training fall apart under life-threatening stress. This has been proven in combat many times.

A deep cover civilian consultant I once knew (I'll call him Jesse) had been retained by a US agency and was working solo in a Latin American country during an extended armed conflict. While there, he contracted typhoid and was laid up recovering for a couple weeks in a remote village. There were guerillas operating in the nearby countryside, but Jesse's cover held and he was not bothered—until he tried to leave.

Thinking he could make his way to a road where he could catch a chicken bus into a town, he set out on foot alone. While walking through the mountainous countryside, he discovered that he was still sick and weak and was afflicted with dizziness and various unpleasant and debilitating symptoms of typhoid.

It was late evening with night coming on and little available light when Jesse arrived at the dirt road where he expected to catch the bus. Four armed men were waiting for him. They were smoking and talking and were as surprised by Jesse's quiet approach as he was to encounter them. The guerillas quickly recovered, brought their weapons to bear, and got off a few rounds, narrowly missing him as he leaped sideways into a thicket of bushes, drew his handgun, and returned fire.

Jesse reflexively dropped into a deep crouch in the bushes, pointed his pistol at the armed men, and emptied his magazine. He quickly reloaded and continued firing. The armed men retreated with much yelling and wild shooting. Jesse ran in the other direction, eventually working his way back to the road a few miles away, where he hitched a ride into town with a Catholic priest driving an old pickup truck. He later learned that he had wounded two of the guerillas and confirmed that they had intended to ambush and kill him because they thought he was an American spy, which in fact he was.

The point of the story? Jesse had served with an elite military unit and a paramilitary unit, in which he had trained in Shooting to Live skills. He had also trained extensively as a civilian in various combat and shooting arts, including the new technique, that was coming into vogue. When he was under extreme stress, the new technique, including the Weaver Stance (a shooting method), disappeared. Jesse had more than a passing acquaintance with the new technique, yet under life-threatening stress he reverted to the simple Shooting to Live method.

A moment before the encounter, he had been doubled over with cramps, his entire body trembling and shaking. He was staggering and stumbling and near the end of his rope. He had lost more than twenty pounds during the previous two weeks. In spite of his condition, or perhaps because of it, he reacted at his most natural, fundamental, and durable level of training and survived.

No one can guarantee how you will perform under stress. But Fairbairn & Sykes and Applegate trained large numbers of men and women in these methods in a relatively short period of time. These same men and women then faced our enemies in World War II. As many accounts show, the methods worked and saved lives. These methods were passed on to my generation and modified in some particulars by some of us, and they still work today.

CHAPTER 14

Defensive Shooting Skills

If you have read chapter 5, "How to Shoot a Handgun," some of this material will be familiar. **Read this entire section before starting any practice.**

THREAT IDENTIFICATION

Advanced perceptual skills for threat identification are beyond the scope of this book. So, for the purposes of this book—an introduction to the gun and its uses—let's take it as a given that you can identify a threat and make a decision to respond with gunfire or to not fire. Sometimes the sight of an armed and determined person will stop an assault. The decision to fire or not is a moral and mortal responsibility and one that no one but you can make at the critical moment. If you want to further develop skills of perception and threat identification, I once again refer you to my book *The Tao of Survival*.

FIELD STANCE

In the chapter 5, I called this position the field stance. Although many use terms such as combat stance, let's stay with field stance. It serves the same purpose and is useful under any field conditions, including combat. It is basically the same for the rifle and the pistol from the waist down. It is a dynamic and powerful position from which the shooter can see, shoot, and move. It provides secure footing and balance for movement over broken terrain and away from or toward an immediate threat.

Basic field stance.

The feet should be at least shoulder width apart with the front foot about a step ahead of the rear foot. The rear foot points straight ahead or slightly to the outside. Both knees are slightly bent. Weight can be shifted from foot to foot without moving. This is a stable and mobile position and allows the shooter to swivel at the waist to engage threats over an arc of more than 180 degrees. This position also allows the shooter to step, turn, and move toward or away from attackers, as well as to cover. This position is similar to the natural crouched fighting stance that many will go to instinctively.

Traversing.

Ideally, the handgun becomes an extension of the hand and arm. With a firm, consistent grip the handgun can point as well as your index finger. About the only difference between the grip for defensive shooting and ordinary shooting is that you should practice gripping the pistol very strongly. This is what you will normally do when threatened.

ONE-HANDED GRIP

Grasp the handgun first with the V formed by the thumb and index finger. This V should be placed as high as possible on the back of the grip and in alignment with the barrel and sights. Wrap your lower three fingers around the grip and grasp firmly, placing most of the pressure toward the rear of the grip. Too much sideways pressure from the fingers can torque the gun out of alignment and lead to missing your target. When practicing, grasp the handgun with as much strength as you can. Continued practice will strengthen the grip.

Gripping the handgun correctly.

One-handed grip.

Arm fully extended with a one-handed grip.

Learn the one-handed grip before the two-handed grip. It is foundational to learning the two-handed grip and, since the great majority of encounters take place at close range, is critical to your defense.

TWO-HANDED GRIP

The two-handed grip, correctly applied, provides more support and stability for the firing hand, thus more accuracy. In defensive shooting, the two-handed grip is best used at distances of three to four paces.

Two-handed grip.

Aside from the fact that the accuracy required from about three to twelve feet does not require a two-handed grip, you may not have your other hand available; it may be engaged in fending off your assailant or pushing a loved one behind your body and out of the line of fire. Also, it takes slightly longer to acquire the two-handed grip, and you may not have the extra tenth of a second if a hostile is upon you.

AIMING AND SIGHT PICTURE

In close-range defensive shooting, keep your eyes on the threat, not your weapon. At close range or arm's length and under immediate threat, there is no time to align the sights with your target and acquire a sight picture. Nor should you take your eyes off the threat. If you can bring your handgun to shoulder level, you can aim simply by looking down the barrel. At close range, you aim by focusing on the threat and pointing. At longer ranges, use the sights as explained in chapter 5 on "How to Shoot a Handgun" but do so quickly. For training, obtain red or orange dots from a gun shop or shooting range to use as focus points, draw a small circle with a brightly colored marker, or use post-it notes or other colored stickers. You can even use playing cards, as I did.

TRIGGER SQUEEZE

The trigger squeeze should be essentially the same as described in chapter 5, with the only difference being that you do it fast.

DRY FIRING PRACTICE

Dedicated and concentrated dry fire practice is even more important in defensive shooting than for sporting use. (Again, more details on dry fire are in chapter 5.) **Before starting live fire, carefully read the all instructions below and practice dry firing from all positions.**

If you can obtain a silhouette target, start with one. If not, draw one on cardboard and cut it out. Place three focus points on the silhouette: one at or just below the waistline of the target, one at the center of the target's chest, and one in the center of the head of the silhouette. Practice at least fifty rounds of dry fire from each position before going to live fire. Do so with intense concentration, as if you were using live rounds.

SPEED

Smoothness brings speed. Practice slowly and be aware of each part of every movement. Practicing in front of a mirror is a good way to make sure you are moving correctly. Speed will come after you have the skill in muscle memory.

DEFENSIVE HANDGUN SHOOTING POSITIONS

The following shooting positions are shown in accompanying photographs.

HIP FIRING POSITION

Hip firing position.

Some experts deride hip shooting as being totally useless. They state that no one can hit anything from this position. Perhaps they are setting their sights incorrectly. No one who knew what they were doing, except a legend such as Ed McGivern or Jelly Bryce, would consider shooting from this position at any distance beyond a couple of paces. Within that range the technique is useful, effective, and may be your only choice if an assailant is at arm's length.

If attacked at close range, the defensive shooter will almost certainly begin to return fire as soon as the muzzle of his weapon clears the holster, or wherever the handgun is carried, whether he or she has trained to do so or not. Therefore, you should practice actually getting hits from this position.

Good hits from the hip can be obtained from arm's length to about two paces or so with a minimum of training. Getting hits from the hip at longer ranges will require considerably more practice for most. Shooting from this position as a deliberate choice at any distance farther than two paces or so is not a good tactical move and will likely result in a miss.

Another reason for using this firing position is that it protects your handgun from an assailant at arm's reach. Extending your weapon will make you vulnerable to disarming. At one time, disarming methods were closely held and not taught to the general public. This is no longer so. Anyone with an Internet connection can view videos demonstrating disarming methods, some of them quite effective. Stick your gun in your assailant's face or chest and he just might snatch it from you and use it against you. Yes, the bad guys watch those videos, too. Also, for example, if you were to go though a door into dark room with your gun fully extended, an assailant could disarm you easily.

In news videos, you may have seen trained military or police entering rooms gun first. Those people have been trained to overcome an attempted disarming, and they have other team members backing them up.

PARTIALLY EXTENDED ARM

Bill Jordan refers to this firing position as the gun-throwing method. This position is more of a true pointing position and is superior to the hip position for getting good hits at, say, three paces, or about nine feet.

Partially extended arm, hip level.

FULLY EXTENDED ARM

This is the most desirable position if your target is more than ten to twelve feet from you. With this position, although your focus will be on your assailant, you will, in essence, be looking down your arm and over your handgun, which greatly improves accuracy.

Fully extended arm.

TWO ARMS FULLY EXTENDED

If you have time to fully extend one arm, you might be able to do so with both arms if your other arm is not occupied. This position provides more stability, greater accuracy, and facilitates transition to aimed fire, which you should use if you have time and the distances are longer than say, fifteen feet.

Two arms fully extended.

Think of all the above positions as points on a continuum. Train to flow from one position to the other and to fire at each focus point as you flow. Of course, in an actual armed encounter you may not need to fire at all. Sometimes the threat of armed response is enough to halt an assault. So, as you train, stay focused on your actions, and do not always fire. Remember, threat identification is a mortal responsibility—one to always keep in mind.

To check if you have a solid position, have a friend push on your hand (or hands) while your arm (or arms) is extended. He or she should not be able to move you or you arm without applying a fair amount of force.

LIVE AMMUNITION PRACTICE

HIP POSITION

Start your practice at one step, about three feet, from your target with your arm down at your side, firearm in hand. The distance does not need to be exact. Bring the muzzle up on target by rotating from your elbow with the elbow tight at your hip or side. Fire with total concentration on your focus point. Note where each round hits. Start by firing one round on the lowest focus point. Bring your hand back to your side. Repeat for ten rounds. Then fire ten rounds, one at a time, on the chest focus point. After each shot bring your hand back to your side.

The idea is to eventually make the process—acquiring the target, raising the gun, and firing—a smooth continuing motion. If your shots are more than six inches from your focus spot or spread out all over the target, check your position and continue to shoot one round at a time until you are getting a group of about three inches around your focus spot.

Then take a giant step back to about six feet from the target and start over shooting one round at a time, ten rounds at each focus point. For most people, this is about maximum distance at which they can get consistent grouped hits shooting from this position.

Hip practice.

Later you will practice the entire flow of shooting from each position and all focus points. But we start with one position at a time.

PARTIALLY EXTENDED ARM OR GUN-THROWING POSITION

After achieving groups at close distances from the hip position, go to the partially extended arm position. Start at about two steps or six feet from the target, which is the maximum distance you used for the hip position. Repeat the same sequence you used for the hip position. Fire ten rounds one at a time on the lowest focus point. Return your gun to your side between each shot. Repeat, placing your rounds on the chest focus point.

If you are getting groups within three inches of your focus point, take a giant step back to about nine feet from your target and repeat. When you get good groups at nine feet, move back to about twelve feet. For most people, this is about the maximum distance at which they can get consistent grouped hits shooting from this position. **Keep in mind the utility of the hip and partially extended arm position is only for close range.**

FULLY EXTENDED ARM POSITION

Start at the longest distance at which you could get good groups from the partially extended arm position—six, nine, twelve feet, or whatever your personal best is. Repeat the process, starting with your gun at your side. Bring your arm up, fully extended, and look down and over your arm and gun to the focus point, then squeeze the trigger. You will find this position to be much more accurate than the previous ones. As before, fire each round with fully focused attention. Place ten rounds on the lowest focus point, ten on the center focus point, and now, ten rounds on the highest focus point. Remember: fire one round at a time, noting each hit and returning your gun to your side after each round.

After getting good groups on each focus point, move back another step, about three feet, and repeat the sequence of fire. Then move back another step, about three feet, repeat the firing sequence. Continue this until you reach the distance at which you cannot get tight groups. This distance varies a great deal, but for most this is somewhere between fifteen and twenty feet.

BOTH HANDS ON GUN, ARMS FULLY EXTENDED POSITION

At some distance—it varies for the individual—while shooting from the previous position, you will find that you can get better groups by using two hands. Whether this is at twelve feet or twenty, this is your maximum effective distance for one-handed fire unless you decide to train more in this technique. With both hands on the gun, looking over the gun and focused on the focus point—not the sights—repeat the sequence of fire: one shot at a time, ten rounds on each focus point. After getting good groups at, say, twelve to fifteen feet, move back as before a step at a time until

your find your maximum distance for accurate threat-focused fire.

AIMED FIRE WITH SIGHTS

Beyond the distance at which you can get good groups using threat-focused methods, you will need to use the sights on your gun. In defensive situations, you must acquire a quick, or flash, sight picture. You can learn to do so by practicing the marksmanship methods detailed in previous chapters, then speeding up the process little by little.

ADDITIONAL TRAINING POINTS

PACING OF TRAINING

Do not be discouraged if you don't get good groups right way. You will if you continue to practice properly. Do not overtire yourself. Take breaks at least once an hour. Few can shoot with full concentration for more than a few hours each day.

A tight three-inch group.

Rest when you find your concentration wavering. It may take you an hour to fire sixty rounds if you are fully concentrating on your focusing point and body position. Shoot slowly and deliberately; this is key. Fully directed attention to your target will give you the best results. Speed will come with practice.

DOUBLES AND BURST FIRING

After you can shoot good groups, say three to four inches, in single-shots from all positions at your maximum distances, go back to closer distances and start shooting doubles and bursts of three to four rounds. To shoot a double, trigger your second round as soon as you have triggered your first round. If your grip, position, and other factors are correct, you will see two holes in your target close to one another, perhaps touching. If your hits are more than three inches apart, check your technique and focus more tightly. This may require a fair amount of practice. Or not. Some get it right away. Once you can shoot consistent doubles, do the same with three-to four-round bursts. When you can hold a group with three-and four-round bursts, you can probably do the same with rapid fire strings of five or more shots. Try it.

The primary reason for shooting bursts is that in reality, no handgun, regardless of caliber, has a great deal of power, and none can be relied upon to stop an assailant without perfect shot placement. This is difficult and sometimes impossible in real-world conditions. Tight focus and rapid bursts may be necessary until your assailant is stopped. By getting more than one round on target, you have a better chance of hitting a vital spot and stopping your assailant.

MULTIPLE TARGETS

After doing all of the preceding training, go to multiple targets. Start over with single-shots at close distance, and traverse from one target to another, as shown in accompanying photos. It's best if your targets are at varying ranges and heights. When you are getting good hits with single-shots, go to doubles and bursts. When you can get tight groups from all positions on multiple targets at your best distance for each position, it's time to increase your speed. Do so gradually and smoothly. With good concentrated practice, you will find that you can shoot about as accurately fast as you do slow.

FIELD CONDITIONS

Next, repeat the same practice in poor lighting conditions, uneven footing, rain, snow, or whatever conditions you are likely to encounter in your environment. When you can get good groups fast in various conditions, you have reached a reasonable level of competence in self-defense shooting. I have seen some students achieve this in one three-day weekend of twelve-hour days. Others required more time, a week or so being more common. Whatever the speed of your progress, do not become discouraged. Remember, thousands of ordinary people, not super athletes, have been trained this way and later prevailed against their enemies.

MOVING WHILE FIRING

The accompanying photos show an advanced student training to move toward assailants while firing, often called running and gunning. The details of how to do this while ensuring that your shots do not go astray and that you are moving safely are part of advanced instruction and cannot be covered here. The photos are included to give you an idea of correct movement and to show why the field stance is fundamental to defensive skills. If you decide to try this on your own, DO NOT attempt this kind of movement with a loaded firearm before you are fully competent in the basic skills. Then, if you want to try this, start on level ground and do much dry practice fire before attempting this with live ammunition.

Pistol run and gun sequence.

Rifle run and gun sequence.

FINAL POINTS TO CONSIDER

There is a good deal more to armed self-defense—more than we can cover in this book. In fact, it would need a separate book to cover all aspects of this topic, as it would for hunting. But these fundamentals will put you on the right path. With diligent and correct practice, you can achieve a level of competence than will serve you well. Of course, no one can predict the results of an armed encounter. You can do everything right and still get wounded or killed.

> **Author's Advice:**
> - Keep your eyes on the threat not on your gun.
> - Point your handgun as if pointing your finger.
> - Look down your arm and pistol barrel if at shoulder height.
> - If using a carbine, look down the barrel.

At the beginning, when you get good hits, pause after each shot and focus on your body alignment—how it feels when you hit where you want. Remember this. The approach I explain in "The Tao of Shooting"(chapter 7) is particularly important in this application. Body alignment, focus, and visualization are all important in training, and should be practiced until they come together instinctively. I recommend that you read that section closely and apply it.

Although you can achieve a basic level of competence in a few days, additional and continuing practice will hone and improve your skills. If you don't have time to go to a place

Correct body alignment.

where you can practice live fire, visualization and dry fire will do a great deal toward maintaining and sharpening your abilities.

A video would reveal that each of the above detailed firing positions is a point on a continuum, starting with the handgun in one hand at or below waist level and ending with the handgun at eye level for the most accurate fire. The defensive shooter should, after mastering the static positions, practice firing from all of these positions as he or she brings the handgun to bear on the target in one smooth, flowing motion. After I learned the basics of these methods, I was taught to shoot a burst during this continuum, as many as six rounds, with the impact point rising with the gun. This was referred to as running a zipper because on a silhouette target, the bullets would strike from below the belt to the head. The idea was that you did not stop shooting until your assailant was neutralized.

We were also taught to move while firing or under fire, sometimes advancing toward the enemy, sometimes getting out of the line of fire, depending on the situation. We were also trained to go to cover, if any, to shoot multiple targets and above all to *fight* with a gun, not just shoot one. This is the mindset you want in defensive shooting.

Keep in mind that while you are firing on an armed assailant, he or she might well be firing on you and hitting you. Being hit doesn't have to take you out of the fight. Remember that it often takes many shots to stop a determined assailant. That can also be true for you. If wounded, you might be able to continue to fire and to fight your assailant. Many have done so and prevailed.

You might note that some of the following photos show protector and principal drills. I cannot teach these skills within the limits of this book, but I have included the photos to give you a general idea of how to approach the problem of protecting your loved ones when confronted by armed assailants. They also illustrate another reason why one-handed shooting is a critical skill.

In sequence:

Protector and principal.

Protector steps in front of principal to shield from incoming fire.

Protector draws and aims toward threat.

Protector controls principal by holding his arm and guiding him to stay behind protector.

Front view of protector shielding and guiding principal while aiming at threat.

In sequence:

Front view of protector stepping in front of principal and drawing his handgun.

Front view of protector and principal with handgun deployed.

Protector with handgun deployed, principal protected and moving.

CHAPTER 15

Guns for Self-Defense

The distances discussed here may seem short. Many choose not to practice at these close distances at all, thinking that if they can score hits at, say, twenty-five yards, they can hit an assailant at two yards with no practice at all. Such has not proven to be the case. This has been shown in hundreds of real-life encounters in which people who had been trained for target-range shooting missed their assailants up close. If learning defensive shooting is your primary goal, you should invest more time in practicing at close range than at extended range.

I recommend that you begin your defensive shooting practice with a .22 target pistol for all the reasons mentioned in the chapter on .22s. I also recommend that you master your pistol by following the procedures outlined in chapter 5, "How to Shoot a Handgun." Shoot your one thousand conscious and considered rounds. Remember, quality counts more than quantity. Accuracy and smoothness first, speed second. You can't miss fast enough to hit your target. Have

some fun with balloons and other moving targets. After this, you will have a firm grounding in the basics.

If you don't want to commit this much time, follow the fundamental methods I have outlined in this section. Once you're confident you have mastered these skills with your .22, progress to a more powerful weapon and start over. If you find yourself missing your mark, go back to your .22 to check yourself. Remember, your .22 target pistol is your no-excuses handgun. If you miss with this one, it's you, not the gun. While learning your basics, you learned to analyze your own shooting. You'll know if you develop a flinch. You'll know how to overcome it. Or, you may elect to stay with a less powerful handgun.

If, for whatever reason, you cannot obtain a .22 target pistol or can only acquire one firearm, use whatever firearm is available to you and practice carefully and diligently. As in hunting, the most important thing is the person, not the weapon.

SMALL-CALIBER WEAPONS

Many competent defensive shooters decide to stay with a small caliber. When I was still active in our martial arts school, we worked with organizations such as the Los Angeles Police Department and the Los Angeles Rape Crisis Center. Our work with the RCC was pro bono—our effort to give something back to the community.

One of our referrals from the RCC was a woman who had been assaulted, held prisoner, and violated in her own home. Clara (not her real name) took our rape prevention class, went on to mainstream martial arts, then into combat classes. Clara was about five-feet-seven, athletic, and hardly a shrinking violet. She worked out with guys who weighed in at more than two hundred pounds and were serious fighters and good martial artists. Yeah, they cut her some slack, who wouldn't? But they worked her hard, knowing that giving her a free pass would be doing her no favor.

After some months, Clara came to me after class one day and said she had come to realize that if a large male with ill intent and similar training attacked her, she probably could not defeat him. After much discussion and training with other weapons, Clara decided to arm herself with a gun. After shooting various handguns at a rental range, she bought a Heckler & Koch P7 9mm—an excellent small, powerful, accurate, and easy to shoot handgun—and acquired competence with it. She could hit playing cards on multiple silhouettes at about twelve feet seven out of seven times—fast.

Then she decided to sell the P7 and buy a smaller pistol.

Her reason was that, given her nightmarish experience, she intended to be armed at all times—in her home, while out and about, and while at work. The P7 was more gun than she could carry at all times with reasonable comfort and in total concealment. She worked in the movie industry as a crewmember. Her job was physical, and often other crewmembers were in physical contact with her while they lifted heavy props and lighting fixtures together. She could not allow anyone to learn that she was armed with a pistol. Aside from the general alarm and gossiping such a discovery would cause, it would most likely result in the loss of her job. In addition, she was not prepared to walk around her own home wearing a holster with a 9mm semiautomatic, and she realized the handgun would do her no good if it was locked in a drawer and someone came through her window, as someone previously did.

Clara settled on a twelve-ounce, palm-sized .25 ACP Beretta as her all the time carry pistol and trained with it until she could hit balloons blowing in the wind, tennis balls hanging from string, and tin cans rolling on the ground. She could draw from deep cover and put two rounds within about two inches on the heads of three silhouette targets from contact range to about twelve to fifteen feet, every time—fast.

I've heard many gun shop commandos say that .25s bounce off heads and are completely useless and that if you shoot anyone with a .25 or a .22, it will just make them mad. Such has not been my experience. And I doubt that any of these bulletproof fellows would care to stand in for Clara's targets. Another factor in Clara's decision was that it was impossible for her, a regular citizen, to get a permit to legally carry a concealed firearm.

In Los Angeles, only Hollywood stars and the politically connected can get permits to carry. If she were going to carry, she had to make sure her pistol was never seen by anyone. She chose to break the law rather than risk a repeat of the most horrific experience of her life. (**I do not advocate breaking laws or carrying a firearm without a permit.** I'm only recounting the decision of one person to protect herself from violation as best she could.)

Some professionals, for example some covert operators and intelligence officers—those not working in war zones—are also armed with small calibers, as are many undercover operators. There are good reasons for this. First, the gun isn't central to their mission. Unlike an infantryman whose job it is to engage his enemy with his weapon, a clandestine operator's mission may be to obtain critical information or an intelligence officer's to recruit an agent of a foreign power. Their orders are often to not engage an enemy with violence unless he or she is threatened and has no choice. Second, they may be placed in danger if their enemy learns that he or she is armed, which in many cases would violate their cover. In this instance, deep concealment is as important as being armed.

The deep cover civilian consultant I previously wrote about, Jesse, was armed with only a pocket-sized .22 in a holster of his own design, which suspended his handgun near his groin, an area sometimes overlooked in first level searches. He also cultivated a non threatening appearance and kept ready cash in his pockets, with which he successfully bribed his way out of danger more than once, preferring the expenditure of a couple hundred dollars to violence. However, there was more than one occasion when he was forced to use his little pistol in self-defense.

One evening at the entrance to his hotel, four men who he knew were members of an urban terrorist group approached him with what he believed was the intention of kidnapping and interrogating him, an experience he would not survive. One of the men openly carried an automatic weapon. The others had handguns, but only one had his pistol in hand—the other two men's pistols were holstered. The men were just beyond arm's reach when Jesse acted decisively and aggressively, quickly drawing his .22 from deep cover and—without hesitation—firing, hitting each of them in the face or head, and dropping all four men instantly. He then fled.

Jesse was successful for a number of reasons: he had an exceptional level of perception, when he perceived danger he acted without hesitation, and he trusted his training and his weapon. Also acting in his favor was the fact that, due to his carefully cultivated appearance and demeanor, his assailants assumed he was not armed and approached him with the confidence that he would be an easy victim. Jesse had no desire to take anyone's life. Nor did he want to get into a full-on firefight, which he was not equipped for. More importantly, a firefight would not have aided his mission in any way. He was tasked with information acquisition and was armed for the sole purpose of enabling him in an emergency to break contact, escape, and evade, which he did successfully. Although his little pistol was instrumental in this encounter, his situational awareness and immediate response were decisive in his survival.

It is popularly believed that only assassins use .22 pistols for antipersonnel purposes. This is mostly, I suspect, because mob assassins are known to use .22s and perhaps because many have seen the movie *Munich*, wherein a fictionalized Israeli *kidon* (assassination) team hunts down the Black September terrorists who were responsible for the deaths at the Munich Olympics in 1972. In fact, Israeli intelligence officers, *katsas*, are often armed with .22 pistols, .32s, or .380s, as are certain US operatives—again, those who are not operating in war zones, where for obvious reasons they would be more heavily armed and wearing body amour. Why smaller calibers in low threat zones?

There are four reasons. First, the smaller calibers are more effective than their size might indicate. Second, the small calibers are easy to learn to shoot well. These are highly trained and skilled professionals, but their profession is not armed conflict, and the chances of them having to shoot to defend themselves are small. They might only receive a few days training and practice with a handgun, whereas they might study a foreign language for years and their cover for weeks in preparation for their duties. Third, the small, lightweight handguns they use are concealable from all but

a close body search. Fourth, the small firearms are not a burden to carry, so the operative will most likely have the weapon with them when and if they need it.

Does Jesse's experience and Clara's decision mean we should all arm ourselves with .22s or .25s, or even .32s or .380s? Of course not. Each of us must make our own decisions and take all factors into consideration. Clara's decision was a personal one. Jesse prevailed due to making the best use of his equipment and training. But the point is that small caliber weapons are not the handicap some experts would have us believe.

One of my training sergeants, Sergeant First Class Poleaski, carried a Colt Model 1908 Pocket Hammerless .380 ACP in a shoulder holster when I met him. He also carried it during his service with the 82nd Airborne Division in World War II and during various irregular actions. He made a nighttime combat jump into Italy, during which there was much confusion with paratroopers spread out over a large area joining into small units with difficulty. Some men fought alone during that night. During this conflict, the paratroopers had only the weapons and ammunition they dropped in with. There was no possibility of resupply until the action was decided and over.

One night when we were getting close to the bottom of a bottle of bourbon, I asked him why he didn't carry a .45. He said, "The .45 is overrated and too heavy, and so is the ammo. I killed Nazis with this little pistol all over Europe. What counts, son, is where you hit them, and that might take more than one round."

Sergeant Poleaski had also been armed with an M1 Carbine, a weapon often criticized as being underpowered. But he thought his weapons were adequate for his needs, and he survived to tell about it. Yes, he knew that the .30-06 M1 was more powerful than his carbine. But the carbine had features that he thought served him better: it was compact and lightweight (which was why many paratroopers were armed with them), it had a twenty-round magazine rather than the M1's eight-round clip, and he could carry much more ammo—the same was true of his .380 Colt.

His decisions may have been decisive in his survival. Many paratroopers ran out of ammo during night fighting after the drop in Italy. After action reports clearly show that many of the causalities from the paratrooper drops and on the beaches at Normandy were due to being overloaded with gear. Some paratroopers landed on marshy ground and drowned; some of the soldiers who assaulted the beaches also drowned due to being overloaded and exhausted. Maybe today's bad guys are tougher and more formidable than dedicated, veteran World War II Nazi soldiers, many of whom had years of combat behind them, but I don't think so. Do you? Really?

Yes, I've heard the stories about the pumped up, steroid popping, amphetamine-driven weight pile monsters. I even have one of those stories myself. But so far, I haven't seen anyone who can flex his pectoral muscles and deflect a bullet. And all the 'roid monsters I have ever seen have had hearts—well blood pumps, anyway—and brains and needed their neurological

and circulatory systems to function, and so will be subject to hits in vital areas, just like lions and tigers and bears.

You don't buy that? You're worried about coming home one night and finding Godzilla in your driveway. Okay, maybe you need to get a Godzilla Gun. But if you do, make sure you master that fire breather so when you touch it off, you hit Godzilla, not some mom out walking with a baby carriage three blocks away. And no, I don't think being able to hit a static target the size of two legal pads at three paces, five out of ten times, using both hands in broad daylight will do it. You'll probably be trying to get out of Godzilla's way, and he's going to be coming at you fast. Why else would be shooting him? You can't shoot the old lizard just because he's eating your shrubbery. It wouldn't be right.

Sergeant Poleaski taught me some blood truths about staying alive, at least one of which later saved my life. And I haven't yet met the expert who has convinced me that power is more important than the ability to hit a vital spot.

If you can master—and I mean master, not just hit a silhouette occasionally—a service pistol and choose to carry one, then, as the Aussies say, "Good on ya, mate." You are well armed. If, for whatever reason, you choose to use a less powerful weapon for self-defense, and you have mastered it, then you are as adequately armed as some professionals. But whatever gun you decide to carry, if any, don't think you have an instant paralyzing ray; no handgun is that. Anything can and does happen during violent encounters, and your choice of firearm might prove to be the least important factor in the encounter. Do not fall into the trap of believing a powerful gun will save the day. All the noise about stopping power and caliber choice is mostly sound and fury signifying not much at all.

"COMBAT" COMPETITION

More than one practitioner of the sport of combat shooting has told me that their sport is "just like the real thing," and the stress of combat competition is like that of an actual firefight. No, it is not. It is not in the same zip code, not in the same city, not in the same country. In the country where death is coming at you, some people scream and cry and void their bowels and bladders, and those are the ones who haven't been shot. Others trance out and empty their guns into the air. Some people revert to lizard brain and shoot everything that moves. I haven't seen much of that kind of behavior at combat matches. I've seen all of that and worse in firefights. So no, the stress is not comparable and the events are not "just like the real thing."

To have it be like the real thing, the shooter would have to be under return fire, which would result in a considerable reduction in the numbers of participants in the sport. I do not foresee such events being organized in the near future. Even the military, which does everything it can to prepare its soldiers for actual combat, does not have its soldiers fire upon each other, nor does it represent that their training is the real thing. In fact, their instructors are quite clear that their training is not the real thing or even close to it. It is, however, the best they can do to train soldiers for actual combat.

Some combat competition can be a good way to acquire skills that would be useful in certain kinds of armed encounters. Other combat competitions are organized as challenging contests, requiring a high level of specialized skills, and have little or nothing to do with any realistic simulation of armed encounters. Shooting sports can be great fun. They provide the opportunity to meet people who share your interest, and they bring with them the stress and pressure of any competitive sport, such as golf or tennis, the desire to win, and so forth. Such sports, if practiced in the right sprit and with the right mindset, can be useful in skill development.

If you would like to participate in these events with the intention of developing skills that would serve you in a real-life encounter, do so with whatever handgun you have chosen to use for self-defense. Do not allow sports enthusiasts to talk you into buying a specialized firearm unless you find that you enjoy the sport and would like to more fully participate. Also, do not be persuaded to buy more gun that you can handle unless you are committed to work up to it. If you discover that you enjoy the sport, then go for it. You'll almost certainly become a better shooter.

There are many local organizations and shooting clubs that offer such competitions. If interested, inquire at your local range. The best-known national organizations are:

UNITED STATES PRACTICAL SHOOTING ASSOCIATION

USPSA bills itself as providing a sporting activity, which although focused on pistol shooting, is similar to golf in that it's a relaxing weekend activity. Its players commonly use highly specialized race guns and fast-draw holsters.

INTERNATIONAL DEFENSIVE PISTOL ASSOCIATION

IDPA presents itself as a shooting sport that simulates self-defense scenarios and real-life encounters.

REAL-WORLD SELF-DEFENSE

There are too many factors in play during any armed encounter to be able to predict the outcome with certainly. An armed adversary may be shot in the heart and continue fighting for some time. Buying a gun and developing good defensive skills does not create a bubble of invulnerability. Biochemistry, individual physical and psychological makeup, training, and determination all play a part. Perhaps more important than guns and shooting abilities are skills such as awareness and perception, the ability to detect intentions and sense a potentially dangerous situation and avoid or deflect the situation before it rises to the level of violence. The decision to go to the gun is one that should only be arrived at after careful situational analysis, which may take place in a split second.

Realize this: in a gunfight, you can do everything right, be armed with the best possible weapon, and still get killed. In the events I relate, the good guys won and their tactics and weapons worked for them. That time. Will those same weapons and tactics work the next time? Maybe. Maybe not. Nothing is certain.

CHOOSING YOUR WEAPON FOR SELF-DEFENSE

It is vital to have a gun you are comfortable with and you can rely on to perform as needed. A firearm that malfunctions at a critical moment can be worse than no firearm at all. Pick a gun with a good reputation, but do not trust it until you have done the drills in the previous chapter and fired a thousand rounds with that particular firearm. Clean and maintain your defensive firearm as if your life depends on it. It might one day.

RIFLES

Centerfire rifles in thirty caliber and above (or any variant, such as .270, .25-06, etc.) have little or no place in self-defense in an urban environment. That .308 with which your neighbor hunts deer can perforate an intruder, the walls of your neighbor's house, and continue on through your walls and strike anyone in its path. In general, large caliber centerfire rifles are far too powerful to be used in the city or a suburban neighborhood.

Springfield M14 chambered for .308, a military battle rifle too powerful for urban self-defense. © Springfield

Further, a rifle does not make a good interior home defense weapon, being too awkward to maneuver in close quarters. Some excellent rifles are made in short versions, but the cartridges are still too powerful for this use. Do not confuse a short rifle with a carbine. Generally speaking—there are always exceptions—carbines chamber a less powerful cartridge than centerfire rifles.

CARBINES

In the United States, civilians do not normally go about their daily business with rifles, shotguns, or carbines in hand. That said, there have been occasions in recent memory when the possession of a carbine would have been most welcome for an armed citizen.

Chambered for less powerful rounds than rifles, carbines are safer than rifles to innocent bystanders. They are more powerful than handguns and far easier to shoot accurately at longer ranges. Although most civilian self-defense needs are at ranges closer than fifteen feet, there have been civil disturbances in recent times when law and civilized behavior broke down and criminals ran wild.

Millions of television viewers witnessed the societal breakdown and violence in 1992 Los Angeles during what was commonly referred to as the Rodney King Riots. Many also witnessed storekeepers and other residents protecting their lives with carbine fire from the roofs and windows of their homes and businesses. Similar disorder and violence followed Hurricane Katrina in New Orleans, although much of it was not captured on television due to the extent and severity of the devastated area, which prevented access by news crews.

I was in downtown Los Angeles the day the riots started and during the following days. People panicked. Drivers ran their cars up onto sidewalks, endangering pedestrians and in some cases, actually running over people to escape traffic jams that confined them to the danger zone. Unarmed people ran to their armed neighbors for protection. And some of those armed neighbors sent out for more ammo for their carbines after they had expended their basic load. Few who saw the firefight between armed citizens and rioters, whether on television or in person, doubt the effectiveness of the carbine.

However, be aware that in close quarter self-defense, such as inside a building, it can be easier to disarm a person with a shoulder weapon than one with a handgun.

There are a variety of carbines currently available. The ones I mention below are those with which I have personal experience.

M16 AND M4

The M16 series has proven its value over the past forty years of use by our armed forces and the militaries of many other countries. Regardless of what you may hear around your local gun shop or range, the .223 (5.56x45mm) round is an effective antipersonnel round when used within its limits. It is not a thousand-yard round. Used within urban ranges, it will do what it is supposed to do if the shooter does his or her part.

More than one version of the round has been issued for armed forces duty, all of them FMJ, which is required by the Geneva Convention. For various technical reasons, there have been problems with some of the duty rounds, all of which have been corrected. As a civilian, you are not limited to FMJ and may choose to use hunting rounds, which are . . . well, let's just say they're adequate for defense. If you've seen what one of these rounds can do, you don't need me to describe it, and if you've never seen what they do, you don't want me to describe it. Trust me on this one.

The longer-barreled models in this series may be a little unwieldy in urban areas, houses, and cars. One of the short-barreled versions would be a better choice for this application. A problem you may encounter with using a weapon from this series is that they are restricted in some jurisdictions as assault rifles. The civilian version is semiauto only and does not meet the definition of an assault rifle, which fires both full automatic and semiautomatic.

Another possible problem is that some of these guns are black in color, and the dreaded black gun may incite unwarranted fear in the un-schooled. On the other hand, that may be a good thing if you're facing a mob bent on violence. In fact, the M16 ballistics can be duplicated in a number of handy carbines in more traditional dress—wooden stock, blued steel, and so on; the Ruger Mini-14 is one of them.

Ruger Mini-14. © Ruger

RUGER MINI-14 SERIES

The Ruger Mini-14, in many variations, has been with us for more than thirty years and has been proven to be a reliable and reasonably accurate carbine. It fires the same round as the M16 series and is equally effective. With a wooden stock, it looks like an ordinary sporting rifle, which in fact it is. It is also less likely to cause alarm among the clueless. The Ruger is also available in a version called the Mini-30, which chambers the Russian 7.61x39 round used in the AK-47. Many states prohibit hunting deer with anything smaller than 6mm, thus the Mini-30 can be used to hunt deer in most states.

AK-47

The Kalashnikov automatic rifle of 1947 is the world's most widely distributed weapon of its type. In military versions, it can be fired either full automatic or semiautomatic. In the United States, only the semiautomatic version is readily available and legal. The standard chambering is 7.61×39.

The AK-47's ruggedness and reliability are well established. Its generous clearances between moving parts enable the gun to function even when fouled, uncleaned, and covered with mud and rust. However, due to those loose tolerances, it is not an especially accurate weapon, as least not in the versions I have fired. I am told that certain current commercial versions are made with tighter tolerances and are therefore more accurate and less tolerant of poor maintenance.

There are many today who like this gun and use it in the semiauto only version. I saw a number of them deployed effectively in Los Angeles in 1992. If you decide to go with an AK, make sure you zero it carefully and understand its limits of accuracy.

TWENTY-TWO RIMFIRE CARBINES

Twenty-two carbines can be effective self-defense weapons in an urban civil disturbance scenario, and they offer many advantages. Nothing is easier to shoot accurately, and nothing is less likely to send wild rounds zinging down city streets and through walls. Twenty-two rimfire bullets can do considerable damage to soft tissue and be effective at stopping assailants. However, they have little penetration through hard surfaces and are unlikely to go through walls, thus making the possibility of hitting bystanders in their homes less likely. Any of the guns mentioned in chapter 1, "The Case for the .22," will do.

SHOTGUNS

In defensive work, shotguns are sometimes referred to as the Hammer because a load of 12-gauge buckshot will often hammer an assailant to the ground. However, this is a result of massive pain and neural overload, not, as many think, from the energy of the projectiles. If you fired a gun powerful enough to knock someone across a room, the recoil would also knock you an equal distance across the room.

For police and defensive use, the 12-gauge with double ought (00) or single ought (0) buckshot is the most common shotgun load. A 12-gauge double ought (00) shotgun shell contains eight lead balls with a diameter of .33, which is to say .33 caliber. A single ought shell contains nine balls of .32 caliber. Firing one of those rounds is sort of like firing eight rounds of .33 caliber or nine rounds of .32 caliber with one squeeze of the trigger.

The question arises: Can you get the same effect by firing a rapid burst of nine rounds from a .32 pistol? Probably not. The massive neural overload from all the projectiles hitting at once produces a more extreme effect. I will note that the Czech Skorpion machine pistol in 7.65 (.32) is much more effective than its caliber would seem to indicate. According to an associate of mine, a Croatian national who fought in the Croatian War of Independence (1991 to 1995) and had more than one occasion to use this weapon in street fighting, a short burst from a Skorpion will reliably drop an armed and determined hostile.

However terminally effective the shotgun may be, it does not make a good interior home defense weapon. As the rifle, they can be difficult to maneuver in close quarters. As with any shoulder weapon at close range, they are more subject to being disarmed. More importantly, unless you have a good bit of trigger time with some kind of 12-gauge, the usual antipersonnel shotgun, it will probably be too much gun for a new shooter to handle, especially for a person of small stature. Even some police departments are recognizing this and allowing smaller officers to qualify with the 20-gauge, a cartridge with much less recoil.

Also, if you fire at a target more than a few yards away, you must concern yourself with stray pellets. A shotgun's pattern spreads as the distance from the muzzle increases. This can result in wounding or even killing bystanders if you were, say, returning fire from your window at urban rioters. If you want to use a shotgun for self-defense, you'll want a short barrel, about eighteen inches, which is available on most of the popular guns. Any short-barreled, semiauto or pump, shotgun will do the job. Some military units are using Mossbergs. Many police departments select the Remington 870. Personally, I have found the Benelli semiauto to be reliable, handle well, and cycle quickly.

Every woman I know who has any experience with both the carbine and the shotgun prefers the carbine. For all but specialized situations, I think anyone is better armed with a carbine than a shotgun.

SELF-DEFENSE HANDGUNS

Obviously single-shot handguns are not a good choice for defense. Repeating handguns are available in automatics and double action revolvers. From least powerful to most powerful, the line up looks like this: .22 or .25 (both of which are at the floor of available power), .32, .380, .38 Special, 9mm, .40, .45 ACP, .357 Magnum, 10mm, and .44 Magnum. I don't consider the .44 Magnum to be a defensive caliber for anyone except the most highly trained and skilled. Anything more powerful is a hunting cartridge.

Which to choose? Generally speaking 9mm, .40, 10mm, .357 Magnum, and .45 ACP calibers are considered service cartridges and the best compromise between power and controllability. However, as I think I've made clear in previous pages, I think the smaller calibers not only have their place but are sometimes a better choice.

I offer somewhat more detail on certain handguns and their use than on shoulder weapons because most will choose a handgun for self-defense. In addition, handguns, by their nature, are more personal devices. Most importantly, people are often given to placing too much faith in them.

SERVICE HANDGUNS, REVOLVERS, AND AUTOMATICS

Revolvers are virtually obsolete for military or police use, but they may be a useful choice for the civilian who only wishes to acquire the minimum level of skill for self-defense and has trouble with understanding mechanical functions.

Many old-timers still like revolvers for self-defense, but for a new shooter, there is little reason to get one, other than if you happen to prefer the revolver's simplicity of operation. This is not to say that a well-used and familiar handgun used for hunting cannot be used for self-defense. But as a service handgun, the revolver's day has passed.

The automatic is easier to learn to shoot well and is much faster thereby allowing more rounds on target. It also holds more rounds and is so much faster and easier to reload that the revolver is not even in the game. The automatic is also more durable, less subject to damage from being banged against a hard object or being dropped, and easier to maintain under field conditions. All these reasons and more explain why automatics are the handguns of choice for every military organization I am aware of and the vast majority of police departments. The universal caliber choice for virtually every military organization on the planet other than a few specialized units is 9mm.

The majority of US police departments use 9mm, .40, or .45. In Europe, the 9mm is now standard for police and in many cases has replaced such rounds as the .380

Two service pistols deserve to be treated to separate discussions. Then we'll go on to the others. Both are single-action automatics and have been around since Moses sent Caleb and his buddies to spy out the land of Canaan—or almost that long.

GOVERNMENT MODEL 1911 .45 ACP

Colt XSE, a variation on the venerable Colt .45 ACP 1911 Government Model. © Colt

Old Slabsides, as the Government Model 1911 .45 Automatic is affectionately known by thousands of veterans and not so affectionately by thousands of others, has been in service for a century. Designed by John Browning, a firearms genius, it has served generations of servicemen and civilians. It's available in a hundred variations, some of which offer match-grade accuracy. It is popular with many professionals for good reasons, including, in most current examples, a clean, smooth-breaking trigger, comfortable ergonomics, reliability (with appropriate maintenance), reasonable accuracy, and good power. But part of the reason many choose this old warhorse is its mystique. It's got major mojo going for it—more than maybe any other handgun.

The 1911 is also available in .38 Super, which I prefer to the .45 ACP, but the .45 ACP is *it*. Many worship at the altar of the .45 ACP 1911 and will have no other handgun. Its devotees will tell you it's the best manstopper ever developed and the best handgun ever invented. It is neither.

One round from the .45 in the foot or arm will not render immediately unconscious every person so shot. It will not put a man down faster than a blast of 12-gauge buckshot in the chest. It is not a lightsaber or a deathray. It has serious mojo, but no real magic. It is simply a good handgun, nothing more or less. But members of the .45 cult will not listen to reason; it's a matter of faith with them.

They will tell you that only the .45 was able to stop charging Moro warriors during the Spanish American War. This is not accurate history, as anyone with minimal research skills can determine. A historical footnote: those charging Moro warriors were often not stopped with Krag rifle fire either. The Army finally settled on using two-man teams to stop those determined warriors—one with a Krag, the other with a 12-gauge shotgun. The 1911 .45 ACP did not even arrive in the Philippines until after most of the fighting was over.

It's a great gun, but if you decide to get one, be sure to learn its manual of arms. I've seen more accidental discharges with the 1911 than with any other firearm. Just getting dialed in on the safeties and getting them into muscle memory takes training, attention, and application. Yeah I know, the gunnies tell us anybody can master the 1911. I've said it myself many times. But many won't. If you're not going to put the work into it, do yourself a favor and choose another handgun.

BROWNING HI-POWER

Browning Hi-Power. © Browning

Also designed by John Browning, chambered for the 9mm, and with a magazine holding thirteen rounds, this was the first high-capacity automatic pistol. The 1911 has good ergonomics; the Browning's are excellent. Many people who handle this pistol say that it's more comfortable in the hand than any other handgun. The Hi-Power's manual of arms is somewhat simpler than the 1911, but in general, the same comments apply. I mention this pistol because it is emblematic of high-capacity 9mm pistols, which leads us to the next topic.

.45 VERSUS 9MM

For the benefit of the new shooter, I will address an argument that has been carried on for years and still goes on in gun stores and at ranges. The members of the cult of the .45 often ambush new shooters and ask, "Why are you using a puny little 9mm when the more effective manstopper, the Hammer of Thor, the all-powerful, the all-mighty .45 ACP is available?" Nine-millimeter users vociferously proselytize for their chosen caliber with various arguments, often aimed at newcomers to shooting.

The two handguns mentioned above, the 1911 and the Hi-Power, were for many years the icons of the opposing camps. Although I have addressed the issue of stopping power, more detail is warranted to forewarn the new shooter. Here in the United States, this notion of the .45 as the ultimate handgun caliber has taken on absurd proportions to the point that a new shooter may be influenced to purchase a 1911 .45 ACP or a 9mm when neither is a good choice. In my view, the controversy is one that accomplishes nothing but the consumption of much paper that could be put to better use. I address it only because it is a heated topic of discussion at virtually every range I have visited in the past few years—much of the heat coming from those who have never heard a shot fired in anger. If I could lay this nonissue to rest, I suspect I would be doing many new shooters a favor.

At Smoke Bomb Hill (the home of Special Forces, i.e., the Green Berets) in the early sixties, I, and most of the guys I knew who were selected for nonuniformed service, selected the Browning Hi-Power over the Colt .45 for our primary personal handgun. We did so for a number of reasons.

There was the feedback from the many men who had much combat experience, both in uniform and nonuniformed service going back to World War II. The consensus was that there was little difference in terminal results in the two calibers. There were also, at that time, a number of engagements in progress that provided immediate information. This feedback was considered particularly pertinent, because some missions required personnel to deploy in civilian clothing and not be visibly armed. Therefore, much weight was given to the importance of the handgun, a weapon normally of little concern on a battlefield. Those deployed in civilian clothing preferred the Hi-Power due to its large magazine capacity and because an individual could carry and conceal more rounds on his person. There were also the results from medical research that strongly indicated that there was little difference in wounding between the 9mm FMJ and the .45 FMJ. Many of the guys deployed in uniform chose the .45 because it was an issue weapon and ammo was available at no cost. In other words, caliber was a nonissue in terms of terminal effectiveness.

"But wait," I hear someone saying. "That's old school. What about now? Everything's different now." Okay, let's talk about now. Now the 9mm is our current handgun service cartridge, as well in dozens of other countries. In fact, the 9mm is virtually the universal handgun caliber choice of military services worldwide. Do you think all those guys all over the world who do this stuff for a living are stupid?

I am in communication with people currently serving in military and civilian service in Iraq, Afghanistan, and other conflict areas. Most of them have been issued 9mms. A few have been issued .45s. None of them have said a word to me about either round being ineffective. A handgun is not a particularly important weapon to a frontline solider, as he is armed with a rifle, carbine, machine gun, hand grenades, and other war weapons. However, a handgun is of the utmost importance to those in nonuniformed service in that it may be their only weapon if they are confronted with a situation where armed enemies grossly outnumber them. Therefore, I consider the conclusions reached at Smoke Bomb Hill back in the sixties, which are also congruent with those in similar service today, to be of considerable importance.

I suspect this so-called controversy is one that started in the pages of hobbyist gun magazines. But whatever its genesis, the discussion has reached the point of absurdity. I was buying some 9mm ammunition in a gun shop recently when another customer said to me, "You better not rely on that 9mm stuff. Get yourself a .45. Everybody knows that 9mm just slips right on through your body without causing any damage."

I did not engage this gentleman in conversation. It seemed hopeless. But my thoughts ran like this, "Slip through my body without damage? Excuse me? Slip through what: my liver, heart, lungs, bladder, spleen, a kidney, through muscles and blood vessels, or maybe it would just slip through my breastbone?" Ask yourself this: just what part of *your* body would not be damaged by a 9mm, or even a .22, slipping right on through it? I don't want any bullet slipping through any part of my body. Enough said.

BRIEF COMMENTS ON A FEW HANDGUNS

I have personally used handguns, although not all models, from all but two of the companies mentioned below. They all make good serviceable, reliable firearms. Your personal selection should be influenced by how the gun feels in your hand, how well it points for you, and how well you can shoot it.

SERVICE AUTOMATICS

The pistols in this category are those used by our armed forces, police departments, and many specialized units. Many nonuniformed professionals also choose handguns in this category for the obvious reasons of superior performance. Service pistols are more powerful, generally have a greater practical range, and carry more ammunition than smaller handguns. These pistols may not be the best choice for concealed carry, but they are the best choice in terms of overall performance. They are not all that hard to master if you make the commitment to do the work and carry through.

Beretta

The Beretta 92 double-action semiautomatic is our current military service sidearm and has been chosen by many police departments. It's reliable, accurate, and a good handgun in almost every respect, although a little large for some hands.

Beretta 92FS. © Beretta

Browning

Browning continues making its Hi-Power, along with a number of more modern designs, all with the exceptional Browning quality.

Browning Hi-Power. © Browning

FN

The 5.7x28 caliber was developed by FN some years ago and is the foundation of their Five-seveN system. This round and the weapons that use it have generated considerable controversy, more in the United States than in Europe, due to its radical approach. In a sense,

this round and the Five-seveN pistol redefine the handgun performance envelope, which is something the militaries of many countries have been searching for. The handgun is now in use with some US police departments, a number of federal agencies, and various European special operations groups.

FN 5.7 in its case.

The Five-seveN uses a small-caliber projectile with a muzzle velocity in excess of two thousand feet per second (faster than any other handgun round) and has a flat trajectory. It is easy to shoot due to the lack of recoil—little more than that of a .22 pistol. From reports I have heard and read, the round produces severe wounds.

I have spoken with people who have used them in action, including SWAT team members, covert operators, and one clandestine agent, all of whom stated that it is highly effective, even devastating, in terminal effect. I have read one second-hand report from a police officer who said the round did not perform for him, and have read a report from a member of a Spec-Ops team who said the round did not perform and required many shots on target to be effective. But the majority opinion, based on a limited amount of respondents, is that this round and pistol is everything it's said to be. Quite a few police officers have privately purchased Five-seveNs for off-duty use.

There have been two topics of some controversy attached to this pistol and its round. The first is that the military duty round, which is FMJ and not available to the public, will penetrate body armor and therefore is a cop killer. This is, of course, nonsense. There are many standard rounds that will defeat body armor. If someone has the criminal intention of murdering a police officer, he or she doesn't need a specialized round to do so. The second point of controversy has to do with the terminal effect of the round. Some simply don't think a small caliber round can be effective, regardless of velocity. We saw the same argument when the 5.56 was adapted in place of the 7.62 and have seen the results. The 5.56 has proven effective in more than thirty years of service.

From my point of view, the round and the pistol appear to have much promise. Although the pistol is about the same size as a Glock 17, it is even lighter in weight and therefore easier to carry. It is more accurate at long range than any current service pistol I have fired and not only in the hands of experienced shooters. Three of my friends, none with more than basic handgun abilities, shooting from a rest were able to consistently hit large paper plates at one-hundred-fifty yards, which is exceptional—extraordinary in fact—and does change the performance envelope of the standard service pistol.

The Five-seveN system might be the greatest thing since the invention of the repeating firearm—or not. Time will tell us more. But one thing we can be certain of is that any metal projectile that strikes you while traveling at two thousand feet per second will purely mess you up.

Glock

Everyone who has been to a shoot 'em up movie knows that Glock makes plastic pistols. Actually, only the frame is polymer. Many, if not most, police departments in the United States have adopted Glocks. The G17 9mm was the first Glock, followed by the slightly smaller G19, and much later by the (sort of) pocket-sized G26.

Glock G19.

The Glock manual of arms is simplicity itself. I have given Glock G19s to one of my sons and one of my brothers-in-law and recommended them to at least a dozen friends, most of whom were not into guns. Glocks are, in some ways, the gun for the person who doesn't care much about guns. They are reliable. They require minimal care. They are reasonably accurate.

Heckler & Koch

H&K is known for making durable, innovative, and reliable guns. The Universal Service Pistol (USP) is a robust example of the H&K approach and is in use by certain units in our armed forces.

SIG-Sauer P226. © SIG-Sauer

H&K Universal Service Pistol. © Heckler & Koch

The H&K P7 is out of production, but it is well worth searching out a used one. Its unique squeeze cocker is about the simplest to use and the safest cocking and safety mechanism I've ever seen. Other than the SIG 210, this is by far the most accurate 9mm I've ever fired with one hundred yard hits on steel plates being common. The P7 is easy to shoot and, with its flat profile, easy to carry.

SIG-Sauer

I don't think I've ever seen a Sig that was anything other than accurate, well-made, and reliable. The P226, an excellent 9mm service pistol, is in use by a number of government agencies, as are the smaller models in this series, such as the P228. The P220 is probably the most accurate .45 ACP I've fired other than specialized custom pistols.

SIG-Sauer P220. © SIG-Sauer

Smith & Wesson

S&W was a pioneer in American-made double-action semiautomatics. They continue production in both steel- and alloy-framed pistols and have introduced a range of polymer-framed guns. Smith is still in production on some of the finest revolvers ever made. Although revolvers may not be service handguns today, if you are not comfortable with any auto and want a powerful handgun, you might want to take a look at the Model 19. I know of no better revolver.

S&W Model 19. © Justin Ayres

Springfield

In addition to their all-steel 1911s, Springfield also offers a number of well-made and well-designed polymer frame pistols. All that I have fired have worked well and been fairly accurate. The grip on the ones I have fired is thinner, therefore for some people, more comfortable than the rather fat-handled Glock.

Springfield Enhanced Micro Pistol (EMP).
© **Springfield**

Walther

I have had no personal experience with any of the newer Walthers, but I am told by friends in the shooting business that they are good guns. I have used older models for more than forty years.

Beretta Model 20s in .25 caliber.

Walther P38. © Justin Ayres

Much vilified by certain experts, the P38 is, in its better versions, a good handgun. The war surplus models required a trigger job to correct its heavy, rough pull; however, those manufactured later did not. The P38 was the first double-action automatic in a service caliber pistol. Most that I have fired have been quite accurate. The P38 is no longer in production, but good used examples can be found.

The direct descendant of the P38, the P5 is an excellent service pistol—highly accurate and compact with good ergonomics. The Walther P88, also out of production, is one of the finest services pistols ever made.

DOWNSIZED SERVICE PISTOLS

There is an ongoing effort to downsize pistols that shoot service cartridges. This is one approach to the more power, less gun problem. I doubt this is really the solution, and I suspect that the answer will come from an unexpected technical development.

POCKET PISTOLS IN SERVICE CALIBERS

Kahr

Kahr pistols appear to be well made. I have never fired one. I mention them here because a number of shooters whose skills I respect tell me they are accurate, reliable, and that they like them very much. I am also informed that the smaller ones, especially in .40 caliber, kick like a Missouri mule.

Kahr K9. © Kahr

Baby Glock

The first baby Glock was the G26 in 9mm; others have followed in larger calibers. I find the G26 to shoot as well as the G19, perhaps a little more accurately. It is shorter in both dimensions, as thick as the larger pistols, so they are not particularly concealable.

There are others. Kimber, Springfield, Colt, and others make excellent quality pocket-sized (if you have really big pockets) versions of their service pistols. If you can handle them and carry them, they might be a good choice. However, they are more difficult to control than the full-sized service pistols.

POCKET PISTOLS

Pocket pistols tend to be considerably thinner than even downsized service pistols, usually lighter in weight, and easier to carry concealed. Being of less power, these pistols recoil less and are as easy to shoot as they are to carry. Excellent accuracy can be obtained from many of them. All of this taken together makes them a good self-defense choice for a civilian who chooses to not carry a larger gun.

This category of handgun is extremely popular, not only with civilians but also with armed undercover or off-duty professionals—and even some gunnies who would be embarrassed if their fellow gun enthusiasts learned that they carried a mouse gun. There's a saying in the shooting community, "Everyone talks .45, shoots 9mm, and carries .380." That's about right, if you include .32, .22, and .25 in the carry category.

Beretta

The Cheetah, available in .22 and .380, appears to be the double-action descendant of the 70 series. Double action is a good thing, especially in a pocket pistol. It offers a greater level of safety and requires more deliberation to squeeze off that first round. As far as I can tell, Beretta doesn't make any bad guns. I have fired a friend's Cheetah. It worked well with no malfunctions and good accuracy.

Beretta 80 Cheetah .22. © Beretta

The Beretta Model 70 series was offered in .22, .32, and .380. A single-action auto once popular with the covert and clandestine community (and still is with some), the Model 70 in .22 became famous—or infamous—as the weapon of choice for Israel's kidon (assassination) teams. Less known is that the Model 70 in .22 caliber was issued to Israel's *katsas* (intelligence officers) as a self-protection handgun. A number of *katsas* overcame a team of Palestinians armed with fully automatic weapons during an attempted bombing at Rome's airport armed with only their .22 pistols. Clearly tactics and aggression were the deciding factors. Hardware rarely is.

One of my best friends, whom I served with for two years, chose the Model 70 in .22 caliber as his personal piece and got excellent service from it. No longer in production, used ones are sometimes available. Beretta makes similar models today in double-action that should serve as well, perhaps better.

Bersa

This Argentine company produces, among other firearms, pocket pistols modeled on the Walther PPK series. Available in .22 and .380, the ones I have fired were reasonably accurate and reliable. The prices and the general quality make these guns a bargain.

Bersa Thunder in .380. © Bersa

SIG-Sauer

The Sig 232 is a top-quality pocket pistol. Available in .380, it fits most people's hands. The ergonomics make the recoil hardly noticeable, even for a small woman with little training. I trained a small-framed woman on the Sig 230, the 232's immediate predecessor. She fired a total of fifteen hundred rounds during training. There were no reliability issues, and it was as accurate as my personal Walther. It pointed well for her and fit her hand comfortably. Not once did she experience sore hands. This may be the best .380 on the market today. You can occasionally find one of the old Sig 230s around but not very often. Those who have them tend to keep them and for good reason.

SIG-Sauer P226. © Sigarms

A variation on the basic Model 36. © Smith & Wesson

SIG P220 Elite Carry. © Sigarms

Smith & Wesson

There are other companies making small-framed, short-barreled revolvers, such as Taurus. But I am most familiar with the S&Ws. Smith makes about a hundred variations on this theme. I can't keep track of them all, but they all seem to be cut from the same cloth, so to speak. Back in the day (as my sons say), I used one and it worked as advertised. But I haven't used a revolver for anything other than hunting for at least thirty years. The small autos offer too many advantages. However, if you're that person who cannot deal with an auto, these little handguns will serve you well within their limitations.

Walther

I bought my first Walther PPK a couple of years before I had ever heard of James Bond and before any of the movies were released. Many think of the PPK as the James Bond gun, but in fact, Ian Fleming equipped his fictional hero with a pistol that was in common use in the covert and clandestine community since before World War II. A double-action semiautomatic offered in calibers .22, .32, and .380, the PP and PPK, a shorter version of the PP, has been in production since 1929.

Walther PPK .22 and other working tools.

The pocket-sized Walther was first recommended to me by a Hungarian Freedom Fighter who had fought Russian tanks with bottles of flaming gasoline in the streets of Budapest. Gabor (not his real name) had also accounted for a number of Russian soldiers with his 7.65 (.32) Walther PPK. I shared a barracks at Smoke Bomb Hill with him and some of his friends who had escaped the Iron Curtain in the late fifties.

One night when we were talking weapons and tactics for urban guerrilla warfare, Gabor said, "I know, I know, in America everything must be jumbo. It is a . . . cultural thing. Cars are jumbo, beefsteaks are jumbo, even women's breasts must be jumbo, and especially guns must be jumbo. But you should understand that it's not only the cowboys with their blazing .45s that know how to employ guns. In Europe we have seen more war, more fighting, more death than Americans can imagine. There are many of us who have done much fighting and know a great deal about firearms from using them in battle."

According to Gabor and his friends, he had killed at least four Russian soldiers in pitched battle, and the Russians were armed with assault rifles and backed up by tanks. How did he do that with his miserable little .32, which most experts today agree isn't enough gun to reliably put down possums at ten paces? Was it simply that Russian soldiers circa 1956 were a bunch of weaklings ready to drop at a loud noise? I've known a few Russian soldiers. None of them were that. And I don't think the ones in Budapest were either. Gabor did what he did the same way hundreds of other unnamed and hard-pressed men and women have survived

and triumphed: with marksmanship, tactics, discipline, and a cool head. He didn't panic. He used what he had and used it within its limits.

I've owned a dozen or so Walthers in the PP and PPK series over the years. The German- and French-made pistols were reliable and extraordinarily accurate. Those made in the United States by Interarms suffer from uneven quality control and are generally inaccurate, unreliable, and will need the attention of a gunsmith before they can be relied upon. Smith & Wesson is now making a version of the PPK under license from Walther. I have not yet tried one and so cannot comment on it.

PALM PISTOLS

Many of the fellows who hang out at shooting ranges and gun shops love to poke fun at these little pistols. You might hear comments like, "Shoot me with that, and I'll get mad and kick your ***," and similar witty remarks. Make no mistake; these little pistols can be deadly.

Intuitively, many people unfamiliar with guns will chose one of these little pistols for self-protection. They do so because they know they will actually carry it every day and will have it when the unexpected occurs. They figure that the little gun will maybe do enough damage to stop an assailant. They aren't wrong.

I am willing to bet that if I could somehow magically shake down everyone across the country, I would find more of these tiny pistols than any other type of handgun, and that's including off-duty cops. More police officers than want to admit it carry one of these or a pocket pistol as an everyday backup or an off-duty gun—when the backup becomes the only gun.

Are all of these people mentally challenged? No, they are not. They made their choice for good reasons. Don't they know these popguns are useless? Actually, they know these guns are not useless. These pistols are appropriate for their environment and threat level.

None of the people who choose these palm or pocket pistols expect to get into running gun battles on their way home from work. Yes, it could happen. But you have to figure the odds. We live in America. We have some areas that are dangerous. We have armed criminals. Muggers and rapists are out there. But get a grip, we don't live in downtown Mosul or Kabul. When was the last time you saw a firefight at your local mall? Mostly what people want is to be able to stop a criminal who is attacking them. At arm's length, a fast three-round burst of .25 or .22 in the face will have a pretty good chance of doing just that.

Beretta

Variations of the 950 model have been in production for fifty years. A single-action auto previously available in .25 (6.35) and .22 Short, the current production is only in .25. Used ones in .22 Short can be found, but they are not reliable. The .22 Short does not feed reliably in these pistols. If you choose a 950, get it in .25.

The 21 model is an updated double-action descendant of the 950 and the discontinued 20 (also a double-action) and is the standard by which other palm pistols are judged. I

have owned both .22- and .25-caliber 20 and 21 Berettas, and they have never failed to do what they were supposed to do. The .22 wants to be fed high-speed rounds, at least mine did. In more than three thousand rounds of high-speed .22, I never had a malfunction. The .25 would handle anything from frangible Glaser or Mag Safe to prewar stuff to current production.

.22 Beretta Bobcat Model 21A. © Beretta

Kel-Tec

The P-32 and the Kel-Tec Company are relatively new to gunmaking, at least compared to Beretta, which has been in business since 1526. I include them here because two of my experienced friends think highly of them and the P-32 is a polymer-framed palm-sized .32 weighing only six ounces. You can even get it with a clip on the side like a Spyderco pocketknife. I haven't fired one yet, but I'm told they are good little guns, though some of them seem to need a bit of after-purchase care. The company has the reputation of taking immediate care of all customer complaints. If you get one of these, be sure to fire at least two hundred rounds with it before relying on it.

Kel-Tec P-32. © **Kel-Tec**

North American Arms

The NA Guardian is offered in both .25 and .32. Both are palm-sized and of high quality. They come without sights, which is fine for 99 percent of the projected uses of the pistol. However, I suspect that these guns are capable of pretty good accuracy at longer ranges.

North American Arms .32 ACP Guardian.
© **North American Arms**

Walther

I've owned six TPHs. Two of them were German-made, the other four were made in the United States by Interarms under license. Unfortunately, the German guns cannot be imported due to legislation. I say unfortunately because my German TPHs have been the best palm pistols I've ever owned, seen, or heard of. With high-speed ammo, they have been totally reliable. On a good day with my German TPHs, I have out-shot friends with target pistols. One-inch groups at twenty-five yards were doable on a really good day, which means hitting button-sized targets at twelve feet was a piece of cake.

None of the Interarms TPHs functioned properly or shot to point of aim. One of them shot twelve inches high at twenty-one feet. Interarms evidenced no interest in correcting the problems. I dumped them with fair warning to a guy who wanted to try his hand at gunsmithing.

TARGET PISTOLS FOR SELF-DEFENSE

What about that .22 target pistol you bought to practice and learn with—can't it be used for self-defense? If you've read everything up to here, you should know the answer. It's the size of a service pistol, so it's no easier to drag around with you. But if you've been practicing, you can probably put ten rounds into a circle the size of a teacup at, say, fifteen or twenty feet in a couple of seconds. What do you think?

BACK UP GUNS

Few civilians are going to go about their affairs toting two guns, nor do I recommend that they do so. I do, however, recommend that once a person finds a gun he or she is comfortable with, he or she buy another one of the same model for a back up in case the first gun goes missing, your pet pit-bull-wolverine crossbreed eats it, or whatever. If one gun goes down, you'll still be armed.

RELIABILITY

Whatever gun you choose, it must go bang every time you pull the trigger if it's loaded. If it doesn't, it isn't fit for self-defense. It's generally agreed that if you can't fire at least two hundreds rounds without any kind of jam or misfire, then that particular gun and ammo combination you're using is unreliable. If I get a malfunction that I cannot immediately explain, I retire the gun until the problem is solved. You may need to have a gunsmith take a look if you're having problems, although sometimes simply changing ammo will do the trick. Either way, correct the problem or get another gun.

CONCLUSION

There is an oft-repeated rule, which is said to be the first rule of gunfighting: Have a gun. It's a good rule, but I don't think it should be the first rule—maybe the second. Here's the first rule of gunfighting according to Ayres: **Don't get into a gunfight**.

The only thing worse than doing violence to another person is to become a victim of violence. There is no moral justification for anyone who would victimize another. However, self-defense and the defense of others is not only morally justified and righteous, it's basic to our humanity. Now, do us both a favor and go back to the beginning of this section and read again my opening comments about the nature of real-world gunfighting. Trust me, this is the first rule: **Don't get into a gunfight**. Self-defense and the defense of others is the only reason to break that rule.